Healing Trauma Through Relationships

The Dignity of the Inner Life and the Gift of Self

David Woodier

Notes About the Book

To protect the confidentiality of individual children, carers, and professionals, names and autobiographical details have been altered. Most stories about young people are composite and drawn from a number of similar examples.

Acknowledgments

I am thankful to:

My wife Jayna who has listened patiently to my ideas and kept me grounded.

My friends Joy and Ed whose advice has been incredibly helpful.

My friends at Scottish Attachment in Action who have helped me grow as a teacher and parent.

Tom Donaldson, artist based in Glasgow, for his sensitive and creative illustrations. @tomdonaldsonart

The young people who have allowed me to share meaningfully in their lives, including the two boys who asked me each week if they could be in my book.

My daughter who keeps me humble: "Dad, you get paid just for being a human being."

Table of Contents

Preface

"Who Made the Waves?   9

Introduction

1 Learning to Respond with Sensitivity to Loss and Suffering   13

2 A Safe Haven in Times of Trouble: Being *Kept in Mind* Makes
   Relationships a Refuge   17

Part I

Responding Sensitively Helps Children Recover Joy in Relationships

3 Matching Affect and Why Dogs Are a Man's Best Friend   21

4 The Gentle Challenge   26

5 Oh No! Not the Thinking Chair   29

6 Parenting Teenagers with Attachment Difficulties   33

Part II

Learning How to Accept Helps Us Stay Open and Engaged

7 Inclusion Can Make Us Better Teachers   36

8 Is it Really a Problem of Self-Esteem? Looking Inside May Not
   be the Answer to How Children Can Flourish   45

9 Balancing the Pencil on Its Point and How We Respond to Anger   49

10 "Change is Hard" A Personal Perspective   55

Part III

Asking to Understand and Being Curious About the Inner Life

11 Verbs of the Heart: Understanding Why We Do the Things We Do   62

12 They Call Me Trouble: The Peril of Not Repairing Relationships   66

13 Emotionally Protecting Children Allows Them to Express Who
    They Really Are   73

14 Understanding Attachment Helps Teachers Build Resilience
    in Young People   77

Part IV

Showing Empathy and Finding Hope

15 The Broken Toilet and the Importance of Attunement   82

16 Wondering Aloud - Building Support for Young People Who
    Are in Crisis   86

17 Noticing the Inner Life of a Child   89

18 Helping Young People Hold on to Hope   90

Conclusion

19 Discovering What Makes Us Human   94

20 The Unfinished Work of Valorising Our Inner Lives   101

21 Epilogue: A Challenge to Christians and an Epitaph to a
    World Come of Age   102

Preface

"Who Made the Waves?"

The elevated train in Chicago, known to the city's residents as the "L," winds its way across some 102 miles of tracks connecting downtown and the lakefront to the sprawling neighbourhoods. This is where my journey begins. Travelling along tracks precariously balanced above the city's streets, two African-American boys, Terry, eight, and Gerald, ten, sat next to me staring transfixed by the view of skyscrapers as we approached the downtown station.

I met Terry and Gerald at a youth centre a couple of weeks before. Newly arrived in the United States, I had signed up to volunteer as a mentor to young people in one of Chicago's toughest neighbourhoods. I remember being invited into their apartment and my shock as I realised that their only furniture was the mattress on the floor and some plastic milk crates that held their clothes. I had no idea at the time that I would spend the next seventeen years living in the inner city, nor how much I would be changed by the children and young people I encountered.

For anyone who has visited Chicago and walked up the Magnificent Mile, the sight of Lake Michigan with its vast expanse of blue water opening up before you is unforgettable. As the lake came into view, Terry and Gerald stopped and a little voice at my side (I forget whose) asked, "What is this?"

"It is Lake Michigan," I replied. But if I was puzzled by this first question, the next question was one of those epiphanies that indelibly marked the significant change in direction that was taking place in my life.

"Who made the waves?" Terry asked.

Although Terry and Gerald lived only a few miles away, that short train journey had brought them for the first time into a world of which they had no first-hand experience. It was at that point, too, I became aware that in order to understand how these two boys saw the world, I would need to cast off my own assumptions. For someone who spent the summers of childhood on the beaches of Cornwall, I still find it hard to imagine the experience of a child growing up in an impoverished neighbourhood in

Chicago, who sees a lake for the first time. It was the beginning of a growing realisation that I would need to question my intuitions about what underlies the

thoughts and behaviours of others in order to understand their perspective and gain their trust.

Terry and Gerald taught me so much. They reminded me that childhood is something to be cherished. Part of the problem, as the author of *The Little Prince* explains, is that "all grown-ups were once children, although few of them remember it."[1] We forget how to see the world in an uncomplicated way; we forget how to look at a lake. I also learned that society viewed young African-American men as having little value. I remember the shock when I heard about their cousin being shot in the back and dying as he lay there on the street. Society only sees boys like Terry and Gerald as an intractable problem. I learned about how hard change can be. I watched helplessly as many of their cousins were assimilated into the street gangs. The gulf between us sometimes felt like a chasm; it was hard for me to build relationships and yet there was something about them that was profoundly worthy of being cherished and nurtured. Like the Little Prince, I just had to learn to see it "without loving it less for being so fragile."[2] Despite the violence and the trauma in the lives of the children and young people in the inner city of Chicago, they helped me see how precious that part of us is that makes us human.

Chicago was the beginning of a journey; I now teach in a large local authority in Scotland. Many of the young people and their stories have a Scottish flavour, but they are not too distant from the lives of the children in Chicago. My work of helping teachers understand how the trauma of abuse and neglect affects children's relationships has taken me on another quest. Some of these articles explore the kinds of fundamental issues I see teachers, carers, and parents wrestling with: How do we respond to suffering and evil? Can a young person really change? How do we value difference? What does it mean to be human and have agency? If we don't at least acknowledge these questions and dilemmas we are at risk of becoming less resilient and of feeling our work is futile and our love is fruitless.

This inquiry has also been driven by a desire for integrity, a belief that my inner life, values, and commitments should find cohesive expression in how I relate to others. A kind of free-thinking individualism has enabled me sometimes to work more creatively. I agree, at least in this point, with John Stewart Mill, who writes: "That so few now dare to be eccentric marks the chief danger of the time."[3] We may be in more peril than we imagine if we separate our personal values from our public lives.

Why do we need a rationale—a moral basis—for our actions toward young people who have been maltreated? Let me answer this first by posing it as a problem. For anyone who cares for children who have been abused, the world appears chaotic and full of tragedy. As if that were not enough, the world also appears hostile to our efforts to relieve suffering. So, on what basis can we have any confidence that our best efforts are indeed not a chasing after the wind?

My confidence comes from my belief that the world in its origin has an overarching purpose and that this gives it an order that is fundamentally good. That order encompasses not only how we treat one another but also things like how children develop from infancy. You would be right in thinking that I can only make these assertions about a good purpose as an act of faith. That is true, but I also believe that such a view of reality—a world that has moral order—allows me to see human beings as uniquely purposed, and it provides a basis for relationships that can be truly reciprocal. (For a detailed discussion see O'Donavan.)[4]

Most of the subject matter here appeared first as a series of blog articles, inspired in part by the threat that I might lose my job during the years of austerity and cuts to public services. I wanted to leave a breadcrumb trail for others who may have a similar role in the future. The added bonus is that in writing these articles I was drawn into a community of many like-minded people who have shaped my thinking and strengthened my resolve.

The chapters are organised into sections that broadly fit within an approach to healing trauma and relationships called PACE: Playfulness, Acceptance, Curiosity, and Empathy.[5] The first four chapters all have something to do with animals, but that in itself doesn't make them playful. Playfulness is not primarily being humorous, but more about expressing joy and interest in being with a young person. It is about helping a young person experience something more positive in their life, even if that is just my delight in who they are. The inner life can be affirmed and celebrated just for the intrinsic act of being.[5]

Learning how to accept a child for who they are means seeing beyond their behaviour. As Dan Hughes says, "We communicate acceptance when we do not judge, evaluate, or criticise our pupil's inner life. What he thinks, feels, wishes, intends, perceives, values, remembers, and is interested in, is accepted as being part of who he is now."[5] In writing the chapter, "Inclusion Can Make Us Better Teachers," I looked at the way teachers were able to show acceptance toward specific young people who were living through distressing circumstances. Communicating our acceptance of a young person's experience without trying to fix their problem may be essential if we are to avoid shaming them.

As we express curiosity, we must be ready to empathise with a young person. There is vulnerability in relationships, especially ones that bring healing. There is also humility. When we are curious about the inner life, we are asking to understand and not assuming we know. We also need to learn to repair our relationship with the young person and accept that no matter how hard we try, they will always be somewhat of an enigma. Empathy also brings us very close to the pain and feelings of hopelessness in children's lives, but it can also be a point from where optimism and hope grow.

Healing from trauma works through relationships that validate, authenticate, and celebrate the inner life of a child. With a trusted adult, a young person can learn that all his behaviours have meaning; even those behaviours that are distressful have some reality that can be shared. For example, validating a young person's anger requires us to be able to listen, to be in the moment, and to acknowledge the truth as the young person sees it. It can also create a dynamic in which a young person can be gently challenged to trust and to accept a new reality. Building trust is the pathway through which the inner life of the child is authenticated: "You can be real, a genuine and unique individual who is loveable and who can bring joy to others." This gift of self comes through self-giving; it is a courageous act that some have described as valorizing the inner life.[6]

This is not about things we do to children; it is more about how we change as adults. For this reason, I have avoided lists of strategies. At the end of most of the articles, there is a section entitled "Keeping it Real." These sections should be used as stepping stones from theory and reflection into practice.

Vulnerability and Suffering

The use of these two words raises important questions. Do we risk victimising and dehumanising young people? Language is a powerful tool that can unmask our prejudices and cultural conditioning, and at the same time allows us to see other viewpoints and can give our arguments greater nuance. I can see the point of view that says that referring to others as vulnerable is stigmatising. Who wants to be defined by their deficiency or neediness? But simply banishing a word or label cannot bring about social justice or change stereotypes. Whenever I use the word, *vulnerable*, substitute something like: "deprived of a significant and loving relationship," and in the place of *suffering*, think: "struggling to find meaning and hope in adversity."

I believe the only way to take away some of the stigma that is real for so many young people who are care experienced is to show that our need for relationship and our tendency to lose hope and meaning in adversity are part of our human condition. In addition, there is a flip side to what society views as a weakness. Our dependency on loving relationships and our hunger to find meaning and hope in life also demonstrates something about our dignity and strength as human beings. I am often amazed at how a young person who has been so badly hurt by the abuse of a parent still seeks loving relationships. We don't give up easily.

In the words of George Orwell, "There is no swifter route to the corruption of thought than through the corruption of language." So allow me the freedom to speak of vulnerability and suffering and trust that I only want to respect the complexity that defines us as human beings. We can be both dependent and strong at the same time, and as one care-experienced person told me: "being vulnerable now is not a death sentence to be vulnerable forever."

References

1. De Saint-Exupery, A. *The Little Prince*. Harcourt Brace & Company: New York; 1971.
2. Gopnik, A. The Strange Triumph of the "Little Prince." *New Yorker. 2014*. Available from:
https://www.newyorker.com/books/page-turner/the-strange-triumph-of-the-little-prince [Accessed April 2020].
3. Mill, J S. *On Liberty*. [e book]. The Project Guttenberg ;2011. Available from:
https://www.gutenberg.org/files/34901/34901-h/34901-h.htm [Accessed July 2021].
4. O'Donavan, O. *Resurrection and Moral Order: An Outline for Evangelical Ethics*. IVP: Leicester; 1986.
5. Bomber, L M. Hughes, Daniel A. *Settling to Learn: Settling Troubled Pupils to Learn Why Relationships Matter in School*. Worth Publishing: London, UK; 2013.
6. Brueggemann, W. *The Covenanted Self: Explorations in Law and Covenant*. Fortress Press: Minneapolis; 1999.

Introduction

1

Learning to Respond with Sensitivity to Loss and Suffering

We are all teachers, and as teachers we operate from some kind of worldview. The meanings and values we attribute to people's behaviour are an indication that no one takes a totally neutral stance. We make assumptions, for example, about why a child misbehaves. We may operate from other assumptions we are unaware of, for example, to what extent we believe a person can change. There is a danger that we approach others without realising how our beliefs shape our ideas, particularly towards young people whose experience in life is very different to our own. What follows in this book is partly my attempt to reflect on my worldview and how it affects my relationships with young people.

This is a record of a personal journey that took me from the inner city of Chicago to teaching young people in the west of Scotland. Along the way, I have been inspired by the healing power of relationships, and I have learned to appreciate the strength of communities when they embrace the full extent of human frailty and difference. I believe that being a Christian has helped me recognise the qualities that uniquely make us human while at the same time helping me overcome my prejudices. I have grown stronger in my convictions that the way we reach out to children and young people should be inspired by a faith that enables sensitivity to loss and suffering in others and an infectious hopefulness about real change and recovery.

There was a spring in my step as I walked from the bus stop to my first school. I felt relieved that I had a teaching job only a couple of days after arriving in Scotland, but I had little idea of what to expect. When the head teacher explained that there were only three children in my class, I thought I had landed on my feet. However, I soon found out that I had a class none of the other teachers wanted. The previous teacher had lasted only one day.

Daniel was nine years old and I quickly realised why the other teachers avoided him, not so much because of his explosive rage, but because of his screaming. When asked to work or to do pretty much anything, Daniel swore and shouted. When threatened with sanctions his distress escalated. His screams echoed through the school and touched a nerve. He sounded like a child being tortured. He had been placed recently with a foster carer, and Daniel was expressing the pain of years of abuse and emotional abandonment.

In contrast to Daniel's diminutive stature, our head teacher was a robust woman whose size and demeanour commanded respect. Her voice had the power of a foghorn. When she walked through the school, I was reminded of one of those great ships launching onto the Clyde River, horns blaring. It wasn't only the children who trembled in fear when she walked the corridors.

There was at least one occasion when I witnessed a softer side to her. Daniel occasionally had contact time with his dad at the school. He would sit next to him in the head teacher's office, inching closer to him and trying to lean into him. His dad sat upright and expressionless; he gave nothing back. Not a cuddle. Not any warmth nor hint of affection.

When Daniel's dad missed their contact time, Daniel emotionally disintegrated. I remember walking back with him from the head teacher's office after his dad failed to show. With no warning, Daniel collapsed to the floor. It was as if someone felled him with an ax. He crumpled to the ground, sobbing inconsolably. It was the only time I ever saw the head teacher visibly moved. She bent down to him and tenderly asked if she could take him home to his foster carer.

Daniel's suffering and the sense of my own inadequacy from not being able to help him troubled me. Early each morning, before my pupils arrived, I prayed in my classroom. I wrote down some of those prayers in a thin blue jotter.

"Father, give me strength not to be afraid or despondent. Please give me love for these young people. I pray they would feel safe in relating to me. In Jesus' name."

I kept asking myself: "What would Jesus do if he walked into my classroom? How would Jesus talk to Daniel?" I conjured up memories, pictures from a Bible when I was in primary school of Jesus sitting and holding a little child on his knee. But Daniel would not have sat on Jesus' knee; Daniel didn't know how to be comforted. I wondered how Jesus would heal Daniel. Daniel's need seemed more complex than, for example, the healing of a fever. I was reminded of one of the most extraordinary miracles recorded in the Bible when Jesus gave sight to a man who had been born blind. Could Jesus use that kind of healing power for a child whose mind was itself sculpted and shaped by the experience of years of neglect? If someone had asked me these questions, I would have struggled to answer. The suffering of others can be disorienting. Answers about why a child would be so badly hurt seem to fall short. Being a Christian means trying to make a difference in a world where some problems, like the suffering of a blameless child, often remain at least partially unresolved.

Even after all these years, I still feel a profound sense of sadness over the happiness Daniel lost as a child. And yet, I am convinced that God is not distant to such suffering. Rather, God allowed himself to be personally affected by human suffering, and that challenges me to follow in Christ's steps. As Dietrich Bonhoeffer, pastor and theologian, wrote before being murdered in a Gestapo prison, "It is not the religious act that makes the Christian, but participation in the suffering of God in a secular life."[1]

I decided to try something I had learned in one of my education classes, a Functional Behavioural Assessment. I kept a log of Daniel's behaviours, describing them in detail but suspending judgements about his intentions. Instead of writing: "Daniel was disrespectful," I wrote: "He pointed his backside at me and hit it with his hand."

Let me point out that perhaps one reason I lasted longer than Daniel's previous teacher was because of my difficulty understanding some of his language. For example, it took me several weeks to figure out what "mon then" meant. (I quickly learned it had the same effect as saying "your mama" to someone in Chicago.) My three pupils fell about in laughter when I asked them what they were saying. To the uninitiated ear, swear words uttered in a Glaswegian brogue may as well be describing some Viking agricultural implement. To be honest, sometimes I just enjoyed listening to their accent.

Over the next two weeks, the list grew. I recorded some thirty distinct behaviours. Each one added to the picture of a little boy in distress. However, something unexpected happened. I found myself able to read him. I could tell by the way he greeted me (or didn't) when he arrived in the morning what kind of day he would have. I knew when he was anxious, and I began to see things about him that were likeable, aspects of his personality I could show him I enjoyed about him.

Gradually, very gradually, Daniel's behaviour changed. He still had times when he raged and tore everything off the classroom walls, but those meltdowns didn't last as long. I learned how to reassure him, "Daniel when you are ready I will help you put everything back on the walls. We can put tape on those posters." (Strange as it may seem, Daniel hated things being broken, and so a lot of tape was used in my classroom.) Other people began to notice a change.

Up to that point, Daniel had not been allowed to go on any school trips. Before I began work at the school, he had gone with his class to a pantomime in a downtown theatre. He had to be carried out of the performance screaming. After a few months of teaching at the school, the head teacher announced that she had now changed Daniel's risk assessment and he was allowed to play football with the school team at an away game, as long as I accompanied him.

A couple of years later, I asked Daniel what was the best thing he remembered about primary school. He didn't say it was having me as his teacher. "Going to the football game and playing with the team," was his reply. What enabled him to cope with the football match? What helped Daniel change? It wasn't something done to Daniel; it probably wasn't any particular strategy. On reflection, I think it was more about my attempt to try and understand him. Daniel experienced another human being reaching out to know him, even in his suffering and distress.

One of the lessons Daniel taught me is that children's development and the harm done by neglect and abuse are profound and complex. They defy simple solutions and dogmatic responses. I needed to be able to adapt what worked by seeking a deeper understanding. I listened more intently to our in-service training; I read more and thought more critically. I needed to be more curious and think more creatively. There were no short cuts or quick fixes. I grew in my role as a teacher; I wasn't there just to transmit skills and knowledge. That could only happen if I learned to take in the perspective of my pupils, and they learned to trust me.

I also realised that Jesus had come to my classroom, but not in the way that I had fantasied. God worked through me, through a relationship. It was in relationships that Daniel had been hurt and it was through relationships that he needed healing. However, I also acknowledge the limitations of anything I could offer Daniel. He needed a relationship in which he would never be shamed or rejected, one in which he would be loved perfectly and given a future full of life. As a Christian, I believe this sort of relationship can be found through knowing Jesus Christ.: "For the Scripture says, 'Whoever trusts in him will never be put to shame.'"[2]

Being a teacher and a Christian is not about presenting Christ as the contrived solution to an insolvable problem. As Bonhoeffer warned, Christ is not the *deus ex machina* who then becomes superfluous once our problems are fixed.[1] I believe my faith in Christ allowed me to feel and share to some extent in Daniel's suffering. I remember one day, Daniel clenched his little fist and raised it up. "I hate you, God!" he shouted. I wasn't offended. Daniel was telling me how he viewed the world. His internal working model could not make sense of how a good God could allow a little boy to be abandoned. To some extent I could relate to his perplexity and even his sense of outrage. I was also in a unique place to be able to gently challenge that worldview and by my compassion and commitment to create a God-shaped space in his world. That space created the possibility that despite what he had experienced, there could be a God who loves him.

Several years later I met Daniel again. I was attending an event at the Council headquarters along with heads of social services and elected council members. A troop of teenagers performed a drama about young people being taken into care. I was dumbfounded as I recognised one of the eighteen-year-olds. For a moment, our eyes met and I could tell he recognised me. Later, I contacted him and sent him a video of a sketch we performed in the classroom. Recalling his laughter when we had dressed up in costumes reminded me of how much he had touched my life. I came to feel something of his suffering, his confusion, and also his joy.

Christians are not unique in wanting to alleviate the suffering of others. We have a sense that the world where children are abandoned and abused is not the way the world should be. Such evil is an intrusion in the created order. In addition, we move towards those who are distressed because we are to take part in what Bonhoeffer calls, "Christ's greatness of heart. Christ experienced in his body the whole suffering of humanity as his own…We are not Christ, nor are we called to redeem the world through our own deeds and our own suffering."[3] I reached out to Daniel because I was convinced of Christ's freeing and redeeming love for him.

References

1. Bonhoeffer D. *Letters and Papers from Prison*. Norfolk, UK: SCM Press; 2017.
2. Bible. Romans 10:11. TLV
3. Bonhoeffer D. *After Ten Years: Dietrich Bonhoeffer and Our Times*. Minneapolis: Fortress Press; 2017.

2

A Safe Haven in Times of Trouble: Being 'Kept in Mind' Makes a Relationship a Refuge

What was your first response when you realised the seriousness of the threat from Covid 19? Did you phone an elderly parent, wonder if you should keep your child home from school, or did you find yourself wanting to escape to a remote spot in the Highlands? I think most of us found our attachment systems going into overdrive. We longed for a safe haven and at the same time to keep those we love safe. It is not easy, because in a moment of fear and crisis we may miss important opportunities to provide reassurance to others.

On one of our recent morning walks, my wife shared this story with me: "When I was a child living in Michigan, I remember the day when tornadoes came through our county. It was a long time ago and I don't remember all the details, but I remember being very afraid when mom and dad told us to go down into the basement. That was the sensible thing to do, but I was still terrified until my dad took hold of me and put me on his knee. At that point, I felt completely safe. We walked on in silence; temporarily flooded with our own emotions. Finally, my wife commented, *"You know a refuge isn't really a place, it's a relationship."*

Before we talk about how we can be a safe haven to others, I think it is important to think more about how the attachment system manifests in adults compared to young children. When Mary Ainsworth devised the strange situation procedure, she found a powerful tool for observing how young children organise attachment behaviours. Ainsworth observed that when a toddler is separated and then reunited with his or her mother, there are clear patterns of behaviour. The child's attachment behaviours, seeking proximity and contact with their mother, could be observed in real time.

In older children and adults, the function of a safe haven and secure base becomes more internalised. How we think about attachment figures becomes more a state of mind, but no less real. Attachment in adults is not so much the sum of early experiences and our attachment history, but how we reflect on and make sense of those experiences, good and bad. John Bowlby suggests the link between early attachment experiences and adults' attachment relationships is not fixed in stone.[1] I think that presents a very hopeful picture. As adults, we are not necessarily victims of our childhoods. We can still pass on a legacy of a secure attachment despite an imperfect past. It is more about how we resolve what has happened, put things into perspective (neither minimising past attachment-related experiences nor being preoccupied with attachment figures), and communicate our love though sensitively interpreting our children's attachment signals.[1]

I think one of the best ways to help children internalise the sensitivity and availability of an attachment figure is by showing that we keep them in mind. I like to explain it like this: I know that several hundred miles away there is a lady, in her eighties now, who probably wonders every day what I, her son, am up to. Most of the time, I don't even consciously think about my mother thinking about me; I just know it. Occasionally, and probably more often when I am worried or stressed, I phone her just to make sure. Being kept in mind helps me have a certain amount of confidence as I go out into the world. When growing up, it allowed me to function more independently. When there is a crisis, the thought of that person's concern for me still provides comfort and a sense of safety and refuge. Now I am older, I still recognise the value of having a secure base and safe haven.[2]

What about the child who lacks that sense of being kept in mind? The foster carer of a teenage girl gave me a piece of good advice about her daughter: "When she withdraws and isolates herself, because she is afraid and anxious, adults tend to stop contacting her. She thinks that if she hasn't seen you, you must have forgotten about her."

It was a penny-dropping moment. For one whole term, she refused to come to school. When I visited the house, she rarely came downstairs to see me, but I kept visiting. I wanted her to get a clear message: *You are not forgotten.*

It must be incredibly hard to be a young person without that default way of thinking that the adults who care about you don't forget you. It must be like living in a world where people fall off a precipice or somehow cease to exist.

Keeping a person in mind often works in an unplanned way. I know of a young person who is adopted, and when his older brother moved away from home to study, he refused to talk about or even acknowledge his brother. One day, quite by chance, while visiting his brother with his parents, he noticed his photograph sitting on his older brother's desk. There was a look of surprise and joy on the younger boy's face when he saw this visible, tangible proof of his brother's affection.

Another adoptive parent remarked, "Even as adults I send postcards when I'm away, especially if I am visiting somewhere we have been together in the past, like a favourite ice cream shop."

At other times keeping in mind has to be more intentional. Some suggestions of how to do this may seem mundane and part of what most people do routinely in order to stay connected. However, the kind of children who need a clear message that they are not forgotten often seem most indifferent or even hostile to an adult's interest. For other young people, circumstances like an unplanned move require adults to make an extra effort.

Sending a postcard during a period of absence or remembering and commenting on a small detail a young person talked about doing over a half-term break can make a difference. As a teacher, occasionally I might ask a young person, "Do you mind if I keep that piece of work on my desk? Every time I walk past my desk, it will remind me of what we talked about today." Even a visit to a home or children's unit is not wasted: "That's okay if they are still in bed, but could you tell them I was asking for them?"

One of the key things I have noticed during the Covid pandemic is how I need to know that I am being kept in mind. A phone call from a friend and an email from a loved one suddenly takes on special significance. Knowing that I am kept in mind also reminds me that in times of crisis, we all feel a need to seek a safe haven. That refuge is not found in a place or an object, but primarily in a relationship with someone you know loves you. There are many metaphors we use to talk about refuge: shielding the vulnerable, standing on a rock, or a chick sheltering under the wings of its mother, but these metaphors stand for the qualities of a relationship with a person who is available and attentive, and whose love is faithful, committed, and protective.

References

1. van IJzendoorn M. Adult attachment representations, parental responsiveness, and infant attachment: A meta-analysis on the predictive validity of the adult attachment interview. *Psychological Bulletin.* 1995; 117(3): 387-340.
2. E. Grossman K.E.Grossman. Essentials when studying child-father attachment: A fundamental view on safe haven and secure base phenomena. *Attachment and Human Development.* 2019:1-6.

Part I
Responding Sensitively Helps Children Recover Joy in Relationships

3

Matching Affect and Why Dogs are a Man's Best Friend

When we talk about putting theory into practice, there is a risk that we think of support as something we do *to* children. Using our knowledge of how children develop secure attachments can help us learn how to attune to them. Expressing curiosity and empathy can be more effective when we learn how to match their affect. In addition to helping children co-regulate, this way of relating can build a special trust between adult and child that may open a door to learning.

The link between trust and learning is often more visible in children and young people who have experienced maltreatment and disrupted attachments. The child who seems to assume the worst about our intentions towards them may also struggle to accept our help or advice. We often experience the young person who seems difficult to motivate or engage in learning as controlling or manipulative. The impression that these children are hard to reach and teach is probably linked to their difficulty feeling secure in relationships.

In the first year of an infant's life, the parent's or carer's capacity to think about what is going on in the mind of the child allows curiosity and empathy about the child's affect*. The carer provides the child with a kind of mirror image reflected in their parent's or carer's face and expression. The child manifests a mood or an emotion to a caregiver, who mirrors it in a display of understood affect. The infant who is crying and distressed sees sadness and distress in his caregiver's face. However, what adults usually do without even being aware of it, is mark or differentiate their display. For example, they may alternate a brief period of making a sad looking face with a soft smile, gentle voice, and rocking. This enables the child to recognise that the affect displayed by the caregiver is a representation of the child's. This secondary representation allows a child to learn to calibrate and regulate his or her response rather than acting it out. [1,2]

Many children who have been maltreated or who suffered disrupted attachments have not had enough experience with someone who can attune and connect with their affect. Yet, being able to experience a consistent, sensitive response from a parent or carer plays a vital role in helping children learn to regulate their emotions. Helping children learn to regulate their emotions when they haven't had these experiences early in life presents us with a challenge. Experiencing an adult who is trying to understand them and give meaning to their behaviour and inner life may be unsettling.

In order to reach out to these children, teachers, parents, and carers have sometimes been encouraged to try matching the affect of the child or young person. This isn't always straightforward, and I have seen mixed results. One teacher said to me, "I try to match his affect when he is upset, but his voice goes up too high."

Another asked, "How do I match his affect when his expression looks frozen or when he curls up in a ball?"

I have also seen teachers amazed at the results when they figure out how to do this. "When I said to him, 'I understand you must be really upset,' he got even more angry. But when I said in a more animated voice, 'I get it! No wonder you are upset if you think you were going to get the wrong answer,' he calmed right down."

Success seems to depend on the child or young person being able to experience what it is like when an adult tries to understand him or her in a curious and empathetic way. It relies on an adult being able to notice the subtleties of a child's expression and relate it to some underlying intention or meaning. This reflective capacity, often referred to as mentalizing, allows us to imagine the fears, desires, goals, hopes, and beliefs that underlie our own and others' behaviours.

Someone who is mentalizing is curious, accepts that their assumptions about a child's behaviour may be wrong but wants to try anyway, is aware of the impact of emotion, and is able to see a humorous side of things. However, mentalizing is also a fragile process. It develops naturally, for example, from the interactions between members of a family, but it can be easily switched off when a child or adult feels threatened or shamed. Similarly, when an adult becomes too rigid in interpreting a child's intentions, when an adult lacks empathy for a child, or even when an adult has lost joy in relating to a child, it may be very difficult to recover that mentalizing stance.

What can we learn from the developmental processes, like mirroring, that can help us learn to match affect? The goal is not to present the child with a facsimile of their expression, but with a copy that is distinctive or marked. By matching the intensity and timing of a child's affect—for example, by matching the patterns of stress and intonation in the voice—the adult demonstrates that understanding of the content of that emotion or mood. At the same time, the adult marks their display; for example, rather than shouting back at an angry child, the adult uses animated gestures. Sadness or disappointment can be matched by the tilt of the head or by an exaggerated sigh. Congruence but with a degree of differentiation allows the child to recognise the displayed affect as their own and not the adult's.

One experienced practitioner explained some of these features in these examples: "So, if a child says to me, angrily, 'I am so stupid!' my verbal response to match affect would be to say in an animated tone: 'That's so hard for you when you think you are stupid!'" I would also match the intensity and pattern in the child's expression with my body language and facial expression. Likewise, if a child was sad and said: 'I am so stupid,' I would say the same words, but my non-verbals would be less animated in intensity in order to match the energy of the child's statement."

The following steps may allow the child to get a sense of "you get me" and "you have understood me." Although our goal is accurate mentalizing (giving the child the picture in my mind of what it is like to be them), we do not have to do this perfectly. It is important that the child experiences the process we use to correct our understanding.

- Build your attunement. Develop your awareness and sensitivity toward a young person. Can we detect subtle change—for example, a different kind of smile—and begin to tentatively give it some meaning?
- Practice listening and being in the moment. Stop telling what is wrong and don't be too quick to offer solutions.
- Practice matching the child's affect. Try to match the energy of the child's emotion, but in a manner that also shows understanding.
- Share your first, faltering understanding.
- Be ready to understand your own misunderstandings.
- Watch how a young person responds when you use wondering aloud**. Use this to improve your understanding of why things are difficult.
- Look for that moment when a young person shows that they recognise themselves in something you have said or shown.
- Be prepared to acknowledge and work with the person when they resist your efforts, without making them feel that they are to blame. "It is hard to work this stuff out. I am sorry I haven't got it quite right. Can you give me another chance?"
- Be aware of what impact a young person's behaviour is having on you. If you feeling threatened or shamed and it is making it harder for you remain open and engaged with a young person, find others who can help mentalize you!

I was in a meeting at a school and one of the teachers, in a light bulb moment, asked this question: "So you mean our job is to help him learn to relate to others rather than give him an education?"

If I could go back and answer that question now, I would say something like, "Actually our job is to learn to relate to him first before we can expect him to relate to us." Yes, relationships are vital to learning. They go hand in hand. It is just that we are used to teaching kids who have learned before they get to school that the knowledge adults have about the world is valuable. For other children, we need to be intentional about helping them learn to trust by giving them opportunities to experience what it is like to have an adult who mentalizes them. That experience of being understood is a key that unlocks learning.[3,4]

This is a true story. Paul (not his real name), ten years old, sits at his desk with his head down. His teacher recognises something is wrong. She knows that the question Paul has been asked may have upset him: "Write about a character in a story who feels rejected." She gently asks Paul, "Come outside with me."

The teacher has prepared herself for a moment like this. She says to Paul, "I can see that it is not easy for you to tell me what is wrong. I would like to do something a bit different. I am going to talk for you."

The teacher continues as if talking for Paul: "If I don't answer my teacher when she asks me what is wrong, I'll get in trouble. But I don't know what's wrong, and I don't know how to tell you." As the teacher speaks her voice becomes more animated and she moves her hands in front of her like the two sides of a closed gate.

She is trying to communicate the sense of frustration, of not knowing, that she imagines Paul is struggling with.

Paul looks up and makes eye contact. Silent tears begin to spill down over his cheeks.

The teacher pauses and then begins to talk about a time when she kept getting something wrong and didn't know how to fix it. She begins to lighten the tone of her voice and Paul smiles.

Later the teacher reflects on what happened. Was she able to match Paul's affect? She can't be sure, but she feels like there was a moment of recognition when Paul made eye contact with her. She thinks that Paul's tears may have come from a sense of relief that someone could talk about him without making him feel ashamed. What is Paul learning? He is at the beginning; this is the first of many moments when his teacher can talk for him. Gradually, he will understand more about himself, and he will see that the emotions that overwhelm him can be understood by his teacher and don't overwhelm her. He can learn that it feels okay when another person helps you regulate your emotional response. The barriers and fears that cause him to back away from learning will seem less because he is learning to trust.

Relating to young people using skills like matching affect allows us to communicate a deeper kind of understanding that can signal to a child that what I have to share with you is relevant and helpful. "If you can get what is in my mind, then I might be interested in what else is in your mind. Now I am interested in what else you have to say about what might work for people in my world."[4]

Experts say that mentalizing is perhaps the most human of traits, and that the animals closest to being able to mentalize humans are dogs. Dog lovers probably already knew this, but it shows what a powerful advantage dogs gain by being able to notice the subtleties in expression of their human owners. How can dogs do this? Try hanging out with humans for several millennia: mentalizing is a great way to build companionship and have someone throw a stick for you.

*Affect is often used as an umbrella term to include inner states that are relatively stable, such as an attitude toward a person and something shorter lived like a mood or an emotional response to a specific situation. It can also refer to something that child is not fully aware of and yet manifests in their expression or body language. If that doesn't confuse you enough, try reading James Gross' explanation in, "The future is so bright I gotta wear shades" Emotion Review 2010: 2(3); 212-216

** The process of wondering aloud is more fully explained in Chapter 16.

References

1. Fonagy, P. What is mentalization? Available from: https://www.youtube.com/watch?v=OHw2QumRPrQ [Accessed November, 2019].
2. Fonagy P, Gergely G. Jurist E., Target M. Affect regulation, Mentalization, and the Development of the Self. New York: Routledge; 2018.

3. Fonagy P, Alison E. The role of mentalizing and epistemic trust in the therapeutic relationships. Psychotherapy. 2014: 51 (3): 372-380.
4. Bevington D. Epistemic trust for AMBIT. Available from: https://www.youtube.com/watch?v=ZBeEOkwLToM [Accessed November, 2019].

4

The Gentle Challenge

For the first two years of primary school, one little girl I know would not talk to her teachers. Even when close friends of the family greeted her, she looked down and said nothing. Although she couldn't explain what was wrong, her dad sensed her overwhelming anxiety. He needed a way to help her change her behaviour, but more importantly, he needed a way to help her realise that being noticed by people doesn't have to be scary. One day he had a small brain wave.

"Here's the deal. People like to see you smile, but you don't like doing the talking. How about when someone greets you, you do the smiling, and I'll do the talking?" The next time Sarah and her dad visited a family friend, they put the plan into action.

"Hi Sarah. How are you?"

"Hello Mr. Duncan," Her dad said. He looked down at the little girl and gently squeezed her hand. She flashed just the briefest of smiles.

Mr. Duncan smiled back.

I didn't know at the time, but this was an example of what Mary Dozier from the University of Delaware calls the gentle challenge. Since then, I have come to realise this is one of the most important goals in building a relationship with a child. As Dozier says, it is about gently challenging their worldview.[1] In terms of attachment, it is a way of helping children revise their internal working model while at the same time avoiding shaming the child.

Children who have been maltreated often have distorted expectations and beliefs about self and others. Bowlby observed that these models are established in the first few years of life. As children get older, they become increasingly resistant to change. "The necessary revisions of model are not always easy to achieve. Usually they are completed but only slowly, often they are done imperfectly, and sometimes not done at all."[2] In addition, adults are too easily pulled towards responding in a way that confirms their existing worldview.

The gentle challenge can only take place in the context of a trusting relationship. This, in and of itself, is a complicated task and one that challenges the young person's view of reality. It is important that the adult can empathise with the young person and has some ideas of what kinds of beliefs and expectations a young person is communicating through their behaviour. The gentle challenge is often used in response to a young person who is showing some kind of resistance to relating to others.

Kai had been moved to a new high school, but the honeymoon hadn't lasted long. He was suspended, and as I drove him home, my mind went back over the years to the little, angry boy I first met in primary school. Kai had fixed ideas about himself and others. When his head teacher retired, Kai told me with all sincerity that he had ruined his head teacher's life. I tried not to smile, but in my imagination I pictured his head teacher sitting in the sun on a cruise ship sipping a glass of something fizzy. Kai was convinced that teachers disliked him, because he believed he was a bad kid.

"Kai how long have we known each other?"

"For years, Mr. Woodier."

"Kai, do you trust me?"

"Yes."

"I need to ask you do something. Can you give some of the trust you have in me to your new teacher? Maybe she doesn't hate you."

Kai said nothing, he just looked at me. I wondered if he could accept that there might be more than one teacher in the world that didn't find him troublesome.

The gentle challenge is often counterintuitive. Sometimes it means joining with the young person in their resistance. We accept that the behaviour allowed the child to survive and cope in an adverse situation, but once a child is safe, we want them to experience relationships in a different way.

"I know it's important for you that I know you are a clever kid. You can keep shouting out the right answers until we work out some other way for you to be sure that I know you are smart."

"I can see you want to be in control of this. I think you are right. I don't think you know me well enough yet. When you get to know me better, perhaps you can trust me to help you."

We probably shouldn't be surprised that children who have been maltreated sometimes give up signalling their need for care and attention. Dozier says it is really important that the parent or caregiver find a way to indicate their availability even when the child acts as if he or she does not need it. In a recent email, Dozier stated, "For example, if a child banged his head and sat alone rubbing his head, the parent might say, 'Oh honey, I'll bet that hurts' while she strokes him on the back." The parent conveys a message: "It is okay to show me who you really are and what you need. There is nothing shameful there."

The gentle challenge is not a clever script; it is a way of building trust and a new way of relating. It often works better when the adult finds a way to do some of the heavy lifting.

"It isn't easy to say sorry to someone you think is angry with you. What about if I do the talking and you just come along with me?"

The gentle challenge often comes as the culmination of months or even years of building a relationship with a child or young person. It is based on an assumption that young people, despite being maltreated, have an underlying need for connectedness and coherence.[1] I see it as a gift, a way of affirming a child just for the intrinsic act of being.[3] It asks children to re-imagine a world in which they can be protected and loved.

One fine day in the middle of summer, I was walking with a teenager around the seaside town of St Andrews. After several expletives (not from me) and a few stares from well-to-do passersbys, I thought it was time for a gentle challenge: "You told me when you are in your class, you need to use that kind of language because you feel threatened. But you are not in class today; you are on holiday, so why not give that kind of language a holiday?"

References

1. Dozier M, Bates BC. Attachment state of mind and the treatment relationship. In Atkinson L, Goldberg S. (eds.) Attachment issues in psychopathology and intervention. London: Lawrence Erlbaum Associates; 2004. p. 167-180.
2. Bowlby J. Attachment and Loss: Volume 1 Attachment. London: PIMLICO; 1997.
3. Brueggermann, W. *The Covenanted Self: Exploration in Law and Covenant*. Fortress Press: Minneapolis; 1999.

5

Oh No! Not the Thinking Chair!

Why do some children find it more difficult to learn from being sanctioned for their behaviour? Do some children think differently? Is it something as fundamental as not being able to see the link between an action and its consequences, or is it more about misunderstanding other people's intentions? When children learn early in life that other people's motives are not always safe or trustworthy, we need a different approach to discipline. There is still a temptation, especially when under stress, that we default to a dogma that children should learn by facing the consequences of their actions.

Consider first what happens when we assume children who have suffered abuse and neglect early in life can change their behaviour in response to being sanctioned.

Thomas was in a Primary 1 class. The nursery had flagged concerns that his language was delayed, and he found it impossible to listen to his teacher unless he was sitting on her lap. Observing him in class was rather like watching a runaway train. When he needed something, he would sprint across the room, knocking over other children left and right. His teacher explained, "We can't have Thomas running over other children. Do you think we should make him sit in the thinking chair?"

A few weeks later, I met Thomas' parents. For the first months of his life, Thomas had been completely neglected. I wondered how he had even survived. Expecting Thomas to reflect on his behaviour while sitting in the thinking chair was unrealistic. What the teacher was expressing was probably her frustration that nothing seemed to get through to Thomas, but what he needed was help at a developmentally fundamental level.

In contrast, John was in his fourth year of high school. He had lived with his gran for most of his life but now she was too frail. John's mother had died of an overdose and his dad was an alcoholic. School reminded John that he was different; he struggled in all his subjects and others made fun of his disheveled appearance. I persuaded the school to let him try horse riding.

On the first day of his lessons, I noticed John watching some of the horses as we drove into the farm. Usually full of bravado, he had become very quiet. He said to me, "I'm nae getting on that thing."

"You need to get on," was all I could think to say.

Two years later, John was still riding each week. Occasionally, I would see the owner of the stables surreptitiously watching him. When John mounted his horse, there was an observable charge of energy flowing between boy and beast. John's riding was now the only thing in his life that was not failing.

The school sent me an email: "Unless John's behaviours in school improve, we cannot let him go riding." The teachers had cause to be concerned about John's behaviours, but even when we pleaded with them, they showed him no compassion.

Compassion is not about showing pity, neither is it purely sentimentality. It understands that a young person does not always have to get what he deserves. Compassion sees his vulnerability and instead gives him what he needs as an individual.

I could tell John knew something was wrong when his foster carer called him into the room. I tried to soften the blow, but John looked crushed when I told him the school's decision. I'll never forget his reaction: "I'm nae going back to school." And he did not. John knew that his behaviour at school was a problem; what he lacked was the motivation to change. He must have felt the whole world was against him.

A basic belief in a benevolent world is not the only thing children need in order to be able to learn from the consequences of their behaviour. A lot of complicated developmental stuff has to have happened. Even in the first twelve months, as Jean Piaget observed, infants, by acting on their environment, learn a huge amount about themselves and the world around them. But is there a limit to how much an infant can learn on their own?

Imagine an infant who sees his favourite toy and extends his hand and fingers towards it. Can we assume the little chap can learn simply by his actions that he can have an effect on his world? Nearly three hundred years ago, David Hume, philosopher of the Scottish Enlightenment was not so sure, and philosophers are still arguing over his ideas. Much of what is happening around an infant is just coincidence; for example, the cat walks past and knocks over the same toy. Even if babies are really good "statistical inference machines"[1,2] and can work out the correlation of two seemingly random events, they still cannot get to what Hume called "necessary connection." We may have no way of grasping how our actions cause things to happen without the help of another person. As infants, we need an interpreter to help work out the consequences of our actions.[3,4,5]

Imagine the same infant who observes his mother reaching out for the same toy. He uses himself as a framework for understanding her actions. "Object-directed, grasping movements can be imbued with goal-directedness, because of the child's own experience with these acts."[6] According to Usha Goswami, Cambridge Professor of Cognitive Developmental Neuroscience, the "like me analogy" opens the door for the young child to learn about his own and other's intentions.[6]

Imagine one more scenario. This time our baby smiles at his mum, sublimely happy that he has found someone to share in his delight. She beams back, her smile not only communicating her own joy but also attributing her child's smile with joyful, generous intentions. The infant has his first lesson in personal agency: "I can bring happiness to others."[7]

As long as that child's interpreter is reasonably reliable and attuned, he or she becomes the gateway for learning about another person's mind and intentions. These are invaluable lessons that can serve him well. What kind of intentions will he attribute in the future to the teacher who gives him a detention? However, if he has grown up with a caregiver who has consistently misinterpreted his acts as apparently provocative, attributing the infant behaviours with a hostile bias, there is good evidence that the same child will attribute the neutral behaviours of others with similar hostile intent[7]. We quickly see that there is a developmental pathway that can have serious consequences for how a child responds to his teachers.

A lot has to happen in order for a child to accurately learn from the consequences of their actions. They need to be able to organise their behaviours around achieving a desired end. They need a sense of their personal agency: "I can bring about something good." They need to have mastered the idea that other people have feelings like them and also act with similar kinds of intentions. (I am still working on that one.) They need to be able to regulate their emotions. Bessel Van Der Kolk concludes, "Predictability and continuity are critical for a child to develop a good sense of causality…."[8]

Keeping it Real

Part of the significant context for a young person is how their behaviour impacts you as a parent, carer, or teacher. These things can feel personal; they can elicit strong feelings of frustration, inadequacy, and being wronged. I have to remind myself that there is no short cut in helping a young person. These are lessons that take time and lots of patience. The skillful part is also about how we present opportunities to young people to reflect on their behaviour. Dan Hughes advises using consequences that logically and naturally follow on from a child's behaviours.[9]

Teachers also have a critical role in helping, even if we have a hard time giving up our sticker charts. But methods based on rewards and sanctions can be modified. I once observed a teacher use a system of rewarding a boy who could become very anxious and dysregulated. She told him that he would need to earn twenty marbles to go on a class trip, but she added, "You will never lose a marble you have earned." I had my doubts at first but in the end, I think it worked because she was sending him a strong message of reassurance.

One secondary school struggled when a group foster home opened in the catchment area. The head teacher regularly suspended a couple of the young people. I suggested he should visit the house and express an interest in them. Kids who have faced a lifetime of rejection need to be reminded again and again that it is about their behaviour and not a rejection of them as a person. "You can't fight in class, but this is your school and I want you back."

Young people, like John, are far more likely to learn from the consequences of their behaviours when we reduce their anxiety and compensate or mitigate for any sense of rejection with clear messages of acceptance. We live in a world where behaviours have consequences and young people look to adults to be competent and fair, but sometimes it seems that compassion is in short supply. We might do well to remember Shakespeare's words that those who administer justice tempered with mercy are twice blessed.

References

1. The infant brain. In our time [podcast on the Internet]. London: BBC; 2010 March 4. [cited 2018 March 28]. Available from: http://www.bbc.co.uk/programmes/b00r2cn4.

2. Sobel D, Kirkham N. Bayes nets and babies: infants' developing statistical reasoning abilities and their representation of causal knowledge. Developmental Science. 2007; 10(3): 298-306.

3. Sobel D. Integrating top-down and bottom-up approaches to children's causal inference. In: Johnson S, (ed.) Neoconstructivism: The new science of cognitive development. New York: Oxford University Press; 2010. p. 159-179.

4. Sakkalou E, Gattis M. Infants infer intentions from prosody. Cognitive Development. 2012; 27: 1-16.

5. Meltzoff A. Born to learn: what infants learn from watching us. In: Fox N, Leavitt L, Warhol J, (eds.) The role of early experience in infant development. Johnson and Johnson; 1999. p. 145-164.

6. Meltzoff, A. Imitation as a mechanism of social cognition: origins of empathy, theory of mind and the representation of action. In: Goswami E, (ed.) Blackwell Handbook of Childhood Cognitive Development. Oxford, UK: Blackwell; 2002. p. 6-25.

7. Goswami, U. Child Psychology: a Very Short Introduction. Oxford: Oxford University Press; 2014.

8. Van der Kolk, B. Developmental trauma disorder: toward a rational diagnosis for children with complex trauma histories. Psychiatric Annals. 2005; 35(5): 401-408.

9. Hughes, D. Adopting children with attachment problems. Child welfare. 1999; 78(5): 541-560.

6

Parenting Teenagers with Attachment Difficulties

As parents of teenagers with attachment difficulties, we may need an extraordinary sensitivity and resilience to stay connected and engaged with our children. It is something we can't do on our own, and yet finding help for adopted teenagers and for those who are in foster care can be difficult. We see our children struggling, but we can't get others to recognise they need help. Sometimes help comes in an unusual form, even from a couple of rabbits.

Have you ever had an experience like this? "Mr. Woodier, what you are describing about your daughter* sounds like any other fifteen-year old."

I feel a wave of despair wash over me. Perhaps this teacher is just trying to reassure me, but it has the opposite effect. My daughter is struggling. Why can't the teachers hear what I am trying to say? I have been trying to get them to understand for years.

In my experience, parenting an adopted teenager is different. I have four children, and my youngest is adopted. All four of them experienced the teen years differently. Although they all faced challenges growing up, my adopted daughter's struggles are more intense. She gets knocked back harder by failure and rejection.

One of the most important things I learned as a youth worker, teacher, and parent is the importance of staying connected, of not letting my children become alienated during those turbulent years.

But that's not so easy because good parenting is a two-way thing. Dan Hughes and Jonathan Baylin, authors of *Brain Based Parenting*, describe this as a kind of reciprocal relationship, "When a mother and her infant feel mutual joy in each other's presence, the infant experiences herself as capable of eliciting Mom's joy, and the mother experiences herself as capable of eliciting her infant's joy."[1] Feeling I have helped my son with a problem or shared a joke with my daughter helps me stay positive, open, and engaged with my children especially when they are struggling. But too often, with my daughter, I am drawn into a conflict, and I am made to feel that I have nothing to offer.

In addition, when I was going through a difficult time with my sons, I could go back and remember what they were like before they became teenagers, the cute and cuddly years. But that is not so easy with my adopted daughter. It has never been easy for her to show love. There isn't so much of a good 'before teenager' time to refer back to.

I try to imagine what life is like from my daughter's perspective. She wants her friends to accept her, but she doesn't want to stand out at school. She wants her parents to respect her as an adult, but she still hugs a teddy bear. She worries what the future will look like and whether she will pass her exams. She can't stop thinking about a boy at school, but she lives in dread that he will find out she likes him. No wonder she seems stressed when she gets home from school.

So as a parent I have to work even harder to stay connected to my daughter. I don't want her to feel alienated or alone. In order to do this, my daughter and I recently became bunny rabbit foster parents. (Yes, there is a charity in Scotland for homeless rabbits). The rabbits also come with strange names. I remember one particularly difficult day, and we were both upset. I said, "Come on. You hold Hey Diddle and I will hold Nuts in May." We sat there in silence for a few minutes. As our stress levels dropped, we began to talk about the rabbits. The angry words were quickly forgotten and life looked more hopeful again.

Parenting my daughter takes every ounce of creativity, patience, and hopefulness I have and then some more. I hold on to every good moment because I know that somewhere in there is a young person who may just need a bit longer to sort out her life. When I get little back that helps me feel like I am a doing a good job as a parent, I need affirmation from friends and family.

So, on behalf of all those parents of troubled teenagers, we know you can't fix everything, but don't minimise what we are going through. We need as much help as we can get during this really important time in our children's lives. Finally, I love my garden but if it helps me stay connected to a very special daughter, I am willing to share it with a couple of rabbits.

*My daughter has given me permission to publish these details. "Dad, none of my friends read your blog anyway."

References

1. Baylin J, Hughes D A. Brain Based Parenting: The Neuroscience of Caregiving for Healthy Attachment. New York: W.W. Norton and Company; 2010.

Part II
Learning How to Accept Helps Us Stay Open and Engaged

7

Inclusion Can Make Us Better Teachers

A tricky but important question about inclusion

The three visitors looked friendly, but what I thought would be an opportunity to showcase our work left us feeling we had been caught off guard.

Someone in headquarters decided it would be good for morale if the heads of education, social work, and health met with some of us who work directly with young people. The initiative was called *Back to The Floor*.

One of the three visitors asked me, "Why should my child's education suffer because the teacher has to deal with the behaviour of a young person who is in foster care?"

I tried to answer, "If I could take you to some of my schools, you would see that schools that are the most inclusive are best for all young people." My words sounded unconvincing. I wasn't prepared, and I couldn't back up my view with any evidence.

Later, I realised that his question expressed a concern shared by many educators. It represents a view that inclusion and achievement are often mutually exclusive.[1] It is a reaction often characterised by simplistic thinking: "Johnny ruins everyone else's chance at a good education." When faced with what seems like an unresolvable dilemma, our tendency may be to look for someone to blame or take responsibility.

Most teachers in Scotland do not have a choice about whether a young person who is looked after (in care of the local authority) and whose behaviour is disruptive is educated in their classroom. As a society, we have placed certain ethical values at the centre of our educational institutions. Schools are expected to protect the rights of vulnerable individuals while at the same time consider what brings greatest benefit to the greatest number. It may seem impossible to reconcile this utilitarian ideal without treating an individual as a means to an end.

In Scotland, teachers are called to reduce educational inequalities by acting as agents of social justice.[2] They are expected to "mitigate the external causes of educational inequality."[3] This is backed by legislation that enshrines a child's right to be educated in a mainstream school[4] and by guidance designed to prevent exclusions from happening in the first place.[5]

Although teachers are expected to embrace inclusion, they often feel they have little help in negotiating the skills needed to build relationships with young people who because of 'external causes' don't readily trust adults or engage in education.[6,7]

The result is that teachers may feel they are caught up in a force field of competing priorities.[6] They are expected to help children attain their potential through acquiring knowledge and skills while simultaneously trying to help a child who is acting out the effects of a history of neglect and abuse.

A more nuanced and relational way of responding to difference is needed. Schools that are both inclusive and high achieving have a different approach to the equity excellence dilemma: they ensure equity by changing the conditions for all learners. Inclusion can be defined as a pedagogy that rather than using specialist knowledge to differentiate for some "extends what is generally available to everybody."[1]

The dilemma implicit in the *Back to The Floor* question helped me understand the need for a conceptualisation of inclusion that could demonstrate a wider benefit. I realised that in order to change attitudes, we need to see the evidence from our own practice that inclusion can provide a better experience for all our young people.

Can you give me one more chance? Inclusion can be transformative

Successfully including young people who are looked after in any kind of mainstream setting can be difficult. Peter was fourteen years old and had been signed up by his foster carer to go to summer camp. It soon became apparent that his carer was under a lot of stress. She said, "I told Peter if he gets sent home, the moment he comes through the door, I will put him in respite care. He has been excluded from school, and people have come to the house to say he is causing trouble in the community. His mum doesn't even want to see him." Peter probably felt being sent to camp was just another rejection. This looked far from promising.

I met Peter as he stepped off the bus and introduced him to his group. He seemed to take a near-instant liking to his group leader, an easygoing and energetic young man. I noticed after a couple of days they were rarely apart. However, Peter was also verbally bullying another boy.

The head of the camp wanted to send Peter back home. "It's not fair on others in the group. He is ruining their week," she said to me.

I asked for one more chance. I needed to help Peter see that he was wanted while at the same time give the rest of his group some time to enjoy camp without the threat of Peter's comments.

I took Peter aside. "We are going to do everything we can not to send you home, but you have to stop bullying. You are going to spend the rest of the day with me and help me clean the kitchens."

After that Peter's behaviour wasn't perfect, but he stopped bullying. A couple of days before the end of the camp, I asked him about his birthday. "I see you have a birthday when you get home. Will you do anything special?"

"No one has ever done anything for my birthday," he replied.

The next day, I was sitting at lunch on the table next to Peter. Without warning, the other young people came into the dining room and sang "Happy Birthday" to him.

Peter looked like a deer caught in the brightness of a spotlight. I think he wanted to run away, but he couldn't. About fifty young people surrounded him.

A year later, we had a call from his foster carer. She told us Peter had looked through the camp brochure until he found the same group of leaders and asked her to sign him up. She told us it had been a much better year at home.

Peter's attitude to camp had changed. It wasn't just one thing that made a difference. His group leader had worked hard to build a relationship with Peter, and the head of the camp was willing to give me one more chance to reach out to him. I believe Peter got the message that he was wanted there.

In the life of a young person who has experienced so much failure and rejection, it wasn't the threat of being sent home that stopped him from bullying.

There was something about being accepted that gave him something to buy into. When he got home, he was still dealing with many of the same issues in his school and community, and yet being included in that camp opened up a possibility that things could be different.

I also noticed that Peter and some other young people who were similarly vulnerable had an effect on the adults at camp. Special effort was made to invite the young people to events during the year. A couple of the leaders made home visits, and the organisers of the camp were keen to invite Peter and others to the camps in the following years.

The leaders and volunteers at camp wanted to make a difference in the lives of young people. By seeing how Peter's situation at camp was resolved, those values were strengthened. We came to camp with perhaps an idealistic notion that the experience would be good for young people like Peter. It was only when those beliefs were challenged and had to be acted on that they became proven values.

This kind of experience taught us that having young people with diverse needs does not present us with unresolvable dilemmas. We grew not only in our convictions but in our sense of agency. We learned that we could work together to accomplish something of value. Paul needed a group of people with diverse experiences and skills. It is only when we express those kinds of social values and skills that we realise our potential: "We define who we are, what we do, and why we do it."[8]

The other campers experienced relationships with adult leaders who they could see were deeply committed to making camp work for all young people, even the most vulnerable. After camp one young person told me that she enjoyed camp, because the leaders made an effort to ensure all the young people felt that they belonged there. Including Peter and some other vulnerable young people communicated a message about the purpose of camp and the value of all young people.

This experience motivated me to consider how I could help other teachers think differently about inclusion. I realised that the experience of successfully including a young person, a turning point experience, might be a powerful motivator for teachers. I realised that teachers would need to master a different kind of approach and set of skills in order to overcome the difficulties of providing relational support to young people who had experienced maltreatment.

A relational approach puts our values into action

"A close, supportive relationship with a teacher is a key feature distinguishing at-risk children and adolescents who succeed in school from those who do not."[9] But it is not only children who are vulnerable that benefit from improved relationships. Improving student-teacher relationships can have positive and long-lasting implications for all young people's social and academic development.[10]

Relationships between teachers and children who suffer from interpersonal trauma are often characterised by conflict. Sometimes teachers respond by becoming less sensitive and more controlling in their relationships with young people.[6] A reflective dialogue with another teacher, can free us up to adopt a more enquiring stance from which we can rigorously question our assumptions and begin to unlock the meaning in a young person's behaviours .[11]

One goal of this kind of reflective approach is to help us interpret behaviour in terms of the child's underlying intentional mental states, their beliefs, feelings, and goals. It allows us to understand, for example, how a child might be responding to perceived threat or uncertainty.

The relational approach mirrors the kinds of interactions that are part of most children's early attachment experiences, for example, having an adult who can read the child's behaviours as communicative cues. Therefore, a key attribute in developing such a relational stance is the teacher's ability to understand the perspective of the young person.[12] However, this kind of insightfulness immediately poses difficulties for some children. It may be experienced by the young person as intrusive.[13] Building relationships with children who have suffered interpersonal trauma needs sensitivity and persistence.

Within the relational approach, the teacher also learns to *gently challenge* a child's internal working models, not by retracing past experiences but by working with the here and now. When done with sensitivity, it can challenge a child's distorted worldview.[14,15] "Do you remember last week? You let me help you sort this out. Can you trust me again to help you fix this problem?"

The relational approach draws on therapeutic practices derived from the theories of intersubjectivity, attachment and mentalization.[16,17,18] It can help teachers think about their communication with those young people, who may be easily overwhelmed by shame.[19]

Our capacity to offer relational support may critically depend on our experience of being part of a network of supportive relationships.[18,20] Taking this approach opens us up to potential criticism from colleagues, who may feel that we should be taking a more punitive approach in the classroom. The relational approach, therefore, as well as having its focus on the adult-child relationship, should also consider how to support the key adult(s) and help them sustain an open, sensitive, and engaged stance. Creating a sense of collaboration and partnership may be vital to engaging teachers in a more reflective type of work.

It is the values and beliefs that shape the culture of the school and the nature of the relationships among its members that are at the heart of practices that encourage both high level of inclusion and achievement.[1]

Evidence: the relational approach can be empowering and inclusive

As the new year began, it had been a steep learning curve for Lewis' teacher. The impulsive and often angry twelve-year-old, who was also struggling in his foster care placement was in trouble almost every week. He was worried about his move to secondary school and had threatened to harm himself. Some of his difficulties and anxiety almost certainly related to the trauma of domestic violence and witnessing the near fatal stabbing of his mother.

Lewis' teacher was one of three teachers in different schools who agreed to meet with me on a regular basis in a relationship-focused, reflective dialogue. They all had children who were deeply traumatised. Brody, nine years old, had suffered emotional abuse after the death of his mother. He refused to work and would run out of class when challenged. His foster care placement had disrupted over the summer. Damien, six years old, was living with temporary foster carers. Teachers reported that he did not like getting things wrong, his behaviour was quick to escalate, and his peers often felt threatened. He spent most of the school day in the depute head's [deputy head] office.

The question I faced was: How can I help these teachers build an attuned, sensitive response to these children? The teachers also expressed concern about the impact of the behaviour of these children on the rest of their class. We met once a week, and we pieced together the clues to understanding each child's behaviour and think about how we could use PACE in our approach.

By the end of the year, the amount of time the children were being educated with their peers had significantly increased. Lewis was no longer being excluded from school, and Damien was no longer sitting in the depute head's office.

Teachers also seemed to grow in confidence. Damien's teacher observed: "My curiosity has given him the opportunity to see that his emotions are not wrong. Before, my whole focus was on trying to prevent him from having any meltdowns. If he has a meltdown now, I am more confident that I can help him."

I also observed changes in the quality of interactions between the key adults and children. When I first observed Brody, he seemed to act as if the teaching assistant (TA) was not there. I wrote in my notes: "He made no eye contact with his TA, didn't respond to her when she spoke to him and ran off several times to try and get help."

In contrast, several months later I observed the following interaction: "Brody blurted out in a queue of children, 'I am going to court.'

TA spoke to him later: You said something that surprised me when you were in the queue, 'I am going to court.' I am wondering if you have been worrying about that?

Brody replied: Yes.

TA commented: No wonder you have been upset. Would you like me to find out more about going to court?

Brody replied: Yes."

The TA was learning how to approach Brody using PACE. By expressing curiosity, empathy, and acceptance, Brody was able to accept her help and feel reassured by her sensitive response.

An important component of the relational approach is the ability of the teaching staff to question their assumptions and become more insightful about how behaviour relates to underlying thoughts and feelings. This helped them respond with greater sensitivity. One teacher commented: "I have learned to make fewer assumptions about the behaviour of other children in my class. I used to think some behaviours were because a child was spoiled at home. I have learned they may have real issues and need my help."

When asked what had made the most difference in supporting Damien, his teacher replied: "I have learned to show empathy. I say things like, 'If I thought so-and-so had done that, I would have been upset.' When I match the intensity of his emotions, he is able to calm down more quickly. Previously, I would have just told him to calm down, but that didn't work."

Teachers commented that they were taking a more reflective stance: "I have been teaching for fourteen years. Damien has helped me more than any other child to think about my teaching."

In applying this kind of relational approach and inclusive pedagogy, staff needed reassurance that they would not be judged negatively by their line mangers if some aspect of work was not going well. After a particularly difficult week for Brody, his head teacher said, "He needs the relationships he has here. He won't have those kinds of relationships if he goes to a special school."

The head teacher also told me that she had spoken to the teaching assistants to explain that his hitting another vulnerable child was more about his own sadness and not just being bad. She was not excusing Brody's behaviour or ignoring the needs of the other child. She recognised that some staff were labelling Brody and that making him feel worthless because of his actions would probably make his behaviour worse.

As part of the work of preparing Lewis' class for their transition to their secondary school, I worked with small groups of his peers. I asked them about their experiences of primary school and how they related to their teacher. They all acknowledged their learning had been held back to some extent by some of their classmates' disruptive behaviours. However, they all had something positive to say about their school: "The work we produce is good and the staff are really friendly." They all rated the relationships in their class as a 4 or 5 out of 5.

One of the group commented on how her teacher had handled pupils' behaviour problems: "She is good at it, because she will sit down and have a chat with them and calm them down."

The children's comments highlight the importance they placed on their relationships and the way that positive relationships can support learning. A teacher's ability to act relationally underpins a more inclusive pedagogy. One of the teachers remarked: "One of my pupils (not looked after) was playing up for another teacher. I used PACE, and I gave him some different options for what might be upsetting him. If I hadn't used this approach, he would never have told me what was wrong."

The TA, who worked so hard to reach out to Brody, wrote this comment at the end of the year: "I have been able to transfer the skills I have learned to help other children. For example, I noticed a change in another child's behaviour. He was getting upset and walking out of class. I expressed my curiosity. I said I had noticed that he was spending a lot of time on his own and that he was distracted easily. I tentatively asked him if the class was too loud or maybe he had a lot on his mind. He said there was too much noise and that it was hard to concentrate. I tried to empathise with him. Later, this child told me he was worried about something happening at home."

The responses of Lewis' peers reminded me of the way that Paul and other young people viewed their experience at camp. They felt they *belonged* there. How we respond to pupils when they are most distressed may signify something about how we value all young people.

Conclusion

Teachers are able to develop an approach that allows young people to experience relationships in a different way, and this kind of inclusive approach requires a more collaborative way of working. Being able to take the perspective of a young person and respond in a more sensitive and attuned way requires a team of people supporting the key adult. In order to think and act more reflectively and to become more insightful about young people's behaviours, teachers require ongoing, relationship-focused reflective dialogue.

Teachers' attitudes to inclusion can change when they experience the difference a relational approach can make. This kind of success may allow teachers to see wider benefits of inclusion. Instead of seeing support for young people who are looked after as taking up valuable resources, the process of learning how to relate to young people can strengthen shared values, bring to life expertise, and define more clearly our purpose as educators. Schools that are inclusive can be excellent, because the skills and qualities teaching staff acquire can enhance what is generally available to all.

Inclusion matters because young people who are looked after find the acceptance they need in order to overcome their sense of rejection and shame. Ultimately, it is through relationships that they can change their behaviour. And to answer the question asked by the *Back to the Floor* visitor, "I would be happy to see my own children in a classroom with the kind of teacher who understands the importance of relationships and finds a way to support the learning of all young people."

What about rights?

Can we use the notion of human rights to solve the kinds of dilemmas that surface when we include young people from troubled backgrounds? As one head teacher said to me, "I am going to get all kinds of criticism from the local community, if I don't exclude this pupil." We look to tribunals to make these decisions, and when children are excluded, we end up with young people who are rarely judged well enough to come back into mainstream settings.

I believe the use of children's rights as a means of building community is flawed in its very conception and pernicious in outcomes. Once we give a child rights that can be legally defended, we have lost the very essence of the goodness of childhood. Children should be able to rely on adults to love and protect them without being defended by law. In the bigger picture, when subjective human rights become the underlying value holding together an educational system, a common sense understanding of children's needs and how children develop is obscured. Our obsession with rights lead us to think of children too much as individuals rather than in relationship. Under the primacy of the right to choose, we feel increasingly entitled, "no one should be allowed to encumber my rights," and we end up with the very thing we wanted to avoid: using others as a means to an end—my end. The legal protection offered by rights may in a limited way restrain evil, but it does not change people's hearts. Political justice cannot truly offer a solution to a moral problem, because it cannot change who we are. By offering young people their rights, we give them a very poor substitute for love.

Keeping it Real: Where are you on the inclusion spectrum?

"I can make a difference in the lives of children who have experienced maltreatment. I may need to change what I do. There is a challenge here but the problem is not the child."

"The needs of this child are beyond what children normally experience. It can't be my responsibility to bring about improvement."

"I can see how the effects of trauma in a child's life impacts how children develop. The potential of this child is not defined by what has happened to them."

"There are limits to how much some young people can change. This child will hold back the progress of others."

"I value input from others to help me think about my teaching. I am actively seeking new ways of working to support learning of all children."

"I am more comfortable working on my own. Others may judge my competence. I tend to trust established ways of working."

Adapted from Lani Florian's *What Counts as Evidence of Inclusive Education* [21]

References

1. Florian L, Black-Hawkins K, Rouse M. *Achievement and Inclusion in Schools*. 2nd ed. London: Routledge; 2017.
2. Scottish Government. *Teaching Scotland's future*. Report of a review of teacher education in Scotland. Available from https://www2.gov.scot/Resource/Doc/337626/0110852.pdf [Accessed 17th May 2019].
3. Pantic N, Florian L. Developing teachers as agents of inclusion and social justice. *Education Inquiry*. 2015; 6 (3):333-351.
4. Pirrie A. Through a glass, darkly: reflections on the 'Presumption of Mainstreaming' in Scottish education. *Scottish Affairs*. 2008; 62(1): 63-79.

5. Scottish Government. *Included, engaged and Involved part 2: preventing and managing school exclusions.* 2017. Available from https://www.gov.scot/publications/included-engaged-involved-part-2-positive-approach-preventing-managing-school/ [Accessed 23 May 2019].

6. De Boer A, Jan Pijl S, Minnaert A. Regular primary schoolteachers' attitudes towards inclusive education: a review of the literature. *International Journal of Inclusive Education.* 2011; 15(3): 331-353.

7. Spilt J, Koomen H, Thijs J, Van der Leij A. Supporting teachers' relationships with disruptive children; the potential of relationship-focused reflection. *Attachment and Human Development.* 2012; 14(3): 305-318.

8. Falk I. Human capital and social capital: What's the difference? *Adult learning commentary.* 2000: 28: October 18. Available from https://ala.asn.au/public/commentaries/Falk1810.pdf [Accessed 13 May 2019].

9. Pianta R, Hamre B, Allen J. Teacher student relationships and engagement: conceptualizing, measuring and improving the capacity of classroom interactions. In: Christenson S, Reschly A, Wylie C. (eds.), Handbook of research on student engagement. New York: Springer; 2012. p. 365-386.

10. Rimm-Kaufman S, Sandilos L. Improving students' relationships with teachers to provide essential supports for learning. Washington, DC: American Psychological Association. Available from http://www.apa.org/education/k12/relationships.aspx [Accessed 17 May 2019].

11.Hart S. *Thinking Through Teaching: A Framework for Enhancing Participation and Learning.* 2nd ed. 2012; Abingdon Oxon: Routledge.

12. Aspelin J. Beyond individualised teaching. *Education Inquiry.* 2014; 5(2): 235-245.

13. Geddes H. *Attachment in the Classroom: The Links Between Children's Early Experience, Emotional Wellbeing and Performance in School.* 2006; London: Worth Publishing.

14. Dozier M, Bates B. Attachment state of mind and treatment relationships. In Atkinson L, Goldberg S. (eds.) *Attachment issues in psychopathology and interventions.* London: Lawrence Erlbaum Associates; 2004: 167-180.

15. Woodier D. The gentle challenge. [blog]. Glasgow: Scottish Attachment in Action blog; 2017. Available from: https://www.saia.org.uk/blog/the-gentle-challenge [Accessed 21 November 2019].

16. Hughes, D. *Building the Bonds of Attachment: Awakening Love in Deeply Troubled Children.* 2006; Maryland: Rowman & Littlefield.

17. Bick J, Dozier M. The effectiveness of an attachment-based intervention in promoting foster mothers' sensitivity toward foster infants. *Infant Mental Health Journal.* 2013; 34(2): 95-103.

18. Bevington D, Fuggle P, Fonagy P, Target M, Asen E. Innovations in practice: adolescent mentalization-based integrative therapy (AMBIT) – a new integrated approach to working with most hard to reach adolescents with severe complex mental health needs. *Child and Adolescent Mental Health.* 2013; 18(1): 46-51.

19. Phillips S, Melim D. Bringing PACE into class. *DDP Canada Conference Proceedings.* 2016. Available from https://ddpnetwork.org/backend/wp content/uploads/2015/01/Sian-Phillips-Deni-Melim-PACE-into-Class-DDP-Conf- Canada-Oct 2014-HO.pdf [Accessed 13 May 2019].

20. Valle A, Massaro D, Castelli I, Sangiuliano Intra F, Lombardi E, Bracaglia E, Marchetti A. Promoting mentalizing in pupils by acting on teachers: Preliminary Italian evidence of the "Thought in Mind" Project. *Frontiers in Psychology.* 2016: 7: 1213.

21. Florian L. What counts as evidence of inclusive education? *European Journal of Special Needs Education.* 2014; 29(3): 286-294.

8

Is it Really a Problem of Self-Esteem? Looking Inside May Not be the Answer to How Children Can Flourish

"A sign of health is the ability to enter imaginatively and accurately into the thoughts and feelings and hopes and fears of another person; also to allow the other person to do the same." Donald Winnicott

Reminding myself to see children for who they can be

When I first meet a young person in school, I like to set myself a challenge. I ask the teacher, "Don't point her out. Let me observe for a while and see if I can spot who she is." Usually I can tell by a child's unkempt appearance, by an argument between two children, or when I see the child who tries relentlessly to get her teacher's attention. However, this simple exercise also helps me think about what a child looks like when he or she is settled and happy. I borrow a metaphor from the garden—flourishing—to describe this kind of happiness in children. A quick search on the internet reveals I am not the first to use this term. The idea of human flourishing has been around at least since the time of Aristotle. However, if we think of flourishing simply in terms of boosting a young person's self-esteem, we may do more harm than good.

Notice me! Rather than low self-esteem, attention seeking may be a cry for mutuality

Nathan's teacher made a discovery and she wanted to share it. "I know what it looks like when he is settled. He isn't looking at me." She must have recognised my slightly puzzled expression and so she added, "I realised that whenever I look at the class, he is already looking at me, but when he is really into something he isn't constantly watching me." Nathan's teacher had nailed it on the head. This little boy was usually in a state of constant vigilance. I remember observing him once responding to conversations happening on the other side of the room.

It wasn't just his hypervigilance that worried his teacher. He constantly sought her attention. He interrupted her lessons, and if that didn't work, he was expert in creating mini-disasters. I have seen water bottles, pencils, and jotters spilled to the floor in a whirl of activity. It would have been easy to think this little boy's problems were all about attention seeking and low self-esteem.

Nathan's teacher came to me one day quite distressed. "Nathan is telling me he is bad. How do I help him have a better self-esteem?" She paused and then added, "I keep telling him he is not bad and that no one is bad, but he told me again, 'Miss, I am bad.'"

I wondered if Nathan wasn't trying to communicate a sense of, "Don't forget me! I can't bear the thought that you don't notice me." Boosting Nathan's self-esteem wasn't going to fix this. He needed empathy; someone who would hear how hurt he was and not reject him. I tried to model a response for his teacher. "Oh, Nathan, if you believe you are bad that must be so hard for you." Rather than attention seeking, a child may be operating from a profound sense of loss, unable to share their grief with others for fear of being abandoned[1].

I have been in many meetings in which a teacher talks about a child who is afraid of failure, lacks friends, has poor personal hygiene, seeks attention, or lacks confidence. It is often thought of as a problem of low self-esteem. What concerns me about thinking in terms of self-esteem is that we may miss not only a child's deeper needs but also become blinded to what true flourishing looks like.

Shouldn't we boost young people's self-esteem?

Not so long ago, the idea of boosting self-esteem was presented as a cure-all for a wide range of social ills such as teenage pregnancy, drug misuse, and other anti-social behaviours.[2] I once interviewed a group of African-American boys growing up in the inner city of Chicago. Naively I assumed they would all have low self-esteem. By the end of the interview, I realised that I was the one with a self-esteem problem. My informal survey surprisingly corresponded to the findings of much larger and more scientific studies. Young people's perceptions of themselves improved significantly during the 1980's and 90's. However, according to some even more rigorous studies that  tracked young people over several decades, improving self-esteem did not reduce drug misuse or risky sexual behaviours. It seems that Bowlby was right to hold self-esteem ideology in contempt for its simplistic reductionism.[2] There are perhaps too many ideas in education that appear to make sense at a superficial level but fail to describe or represent the complexity of human beings.

The wounded self may mask its true needs

I don't want to minimise the depth of harm caused to a child who suffers maltreatment or the devastating impact that neglect and abuse can have on a child's developing sense of self. An infant's earliest experience of intimacy with another human being should be one of safety and security. It is in that state of dependence that the infant should be able to experience a sense of rightness and wholeness about themselves. When safety, security, and continuity of care are lacking, a child may suffer a primal, narcissistic wound.[1]

Put simply, we were not built to flourish as separated beings, so recovery shouldn't be thought of as boosting self-esteem. Rather, a young person needs to experience relationships in which he or she can be free from a preoccupation with self. Donald Winnicott warned that a child may develop a *false self* as a way of masking their true need for mutuality*.[3,4] I think children and young people are happier when they experience the freedom of self-forgetfulness; instead of using a false self to protect themselves, they are able to experience an integrity of self. Again, put simply, they can enjoy other people enjoying being with them.

Not being preoccupied with self allowed him to enjoy being with his classmates

Several years later, in another school and with another teacher, I walked in to Nathan's classroom and for a moment I couldn't see him. He was reading a book with two other

children. They were peering down at the pages, each with his or her chin cupped in hands. Nathan seemed totally absorbed in the moment. So much so that even his posture was a mirror image of the two other children. I am not being unrealistic; I didn't think for one moment that Nathan would never struggle again. However, this little glimpse of Nathan being able to relate to others in a way in which he could express his comfort with just being himself helped me think of him not just as an injured, traumatised little boy.

Human flourishing as having the freedom to forget self

For the past thirty years, I have taken young people to summer camp. This year was no exception. Driving back from a day trip, my car was packed with teenagers. Someone asked to play music from *Les Miserables*. The young people sang along at the top of their lungs, but one voice stood out to me, not because it was louder but because I had never heard that young person singing before. A young man, one of my pupils, who has lived in fourteen different homes and suffered relentless rejection and loss. He wasn't trying to draw attention to himself; he was just enjoying being part of the group. For a few moments, I was reminded of what it looks like when young people are flourishing. I find that I never stop needing to be reminded of what that looks like.

Keeping It Real

1. What do we really mean when we say a child has low self-esteem?

2. What other needs might the child be trying to communicate?

3. How do I refresh my vision of what it looks like when children are truly flourishing?

* Mutuality can be defined as an empathetic exchange between a child and an adult that communicates a sense of being understood. The child's thoughts and feelings are matched in intensity of involvement and interest.[5] Donald Winnicott gave this example: "Settled in for a feed, the baby looks at the mother's face and his or her hand reaches up so that in play the baby is feeding the mother by means of a finger in the mouth … The baby whose mother is involved in this intense identification with him benefits from the experience of feeling understood."[4]

References

1. Newton Verrier N. The Primal Wound: Understanding the Adopted Child. Coram BAAF; 2009.

2. Harrison G. The Big Ego Trip: Finding True Significance in a Culture of Self-Esteem. Nottingham: Intervarsity Press; 2013.

3. Phillips A. Winnicott. London: Fontana Press;1988.

4. Abram J. The Language of Winnicott: A Dictionary of Winnicott's Use of Words. 2nd ed. London: Karnac; 2007.

5.Jordan J V. The meaning of mutuality. Wellesley Centres for Women; 1986. Available from: https://www.wcwonline.org/vmfiles/23sc.pdf [Accessed 2/10/2017].

9

"Balancing the Pencil on its Point" and how we Respond to Anger

"His rage was his worriment" Lewis Grassic Gibbon

"Mr. Woodier, I have anger issues. My French teacher shouted at me. I swore at her and walked out." Mairi seemed visibly shaken. The tone of her voice wasn't defiant; it sounded more like a plea for help.

The obvious remedy for such an outburst is a dose of anger management, or is it? When a young person's anger is seen as a threat to others, the context and reasons for that anger can easily be overlooked. Do our cognitive-behavioural strategies even work, or do we risk increasing the experience of victimisation in some children's lives? Schools may inadvertently pathologise anger instead of seeing how it can be a constructive and healing force.

Mairi was in second year of high school. When I first met her she was only five years old, and she spent most of the school day sitting on her teacher's lap or under a classroom table. Her behaviour seesawed between angry outbursts and emotional shutdown. When she came to me and told me about her outburst in French, I wondered how I could help her see that the reason for her anger wasn't coming from some kind of psychological weakness or flaw.

I can probably mark out my career by various failed attempts at addressing anger and aggression. Twenty years ago, I remember driving a minibus on Interstate 94 north of Chicago. We weren't even out of the city limits and a fight broke out among the half dozen boys in the back. When in school, they were grouped in a class for what was called back then behaviourally disordered children. In other words, in a neighbourhood and school renowned for crime and gang violence, this merry band had been labelled the most violent and aggressive. We had practiced our anger management skills for weeks, but it was back to the drawing board for me.

Anger management has become part of what Val Gillies calls the *new orthodoxy of emotion*.[1] Uncontrolled emotionality is seen as a threat to learning, and pupils are taught how to abstract feelings in order to better manage them. Schools are expected to teach emotional and social skills. These things may sound admirable, until we look more closely.

Gillies' work in three inner city schools in London found that real issues around justice and power relations were obscured. Rather than using expressions of emotion to explore these issues, emotional responses like anger, outrage, or hurt were detached from the circumstances that provoked them. In addition, judgements of right and wrong left little room for teachers to engage with alternative moral frameworks without misinterpreting or pathologising them. Entirely missing was an understanding of the relational dynamics shaping the acting out of emotions. "The challenging behaviour we encountered was more often associated with social connectedness than its absence. Breeched social codes, personal loyalty, and misplaced humour tended to drive confrontations."[1]

Back in Chicago, instead of focusing on anger management skills, I gave each boy instruction on a skill they could use on our next adventure. I taught one how to recognise snakes, another how to take photographs, and another how to cook on a camp stove. The time came for our next trip. This time we made it all the way to the Wisconsin River. Before we set out in our canoes, we went climbing on one of the bluffs along the river. As I describe what happened next, remember these were city kids, and they had never been out of their urban environment. Back in their neighbourhood, every day was about survival. Most had older brothers who were gang members. Threat was everywhere, and status and reputation for fighting meant everything.

The first boy, Justin, short but muscular and bristling with bravado, stepped up to the cliff face. Half way up, he froze. Something was wrong. He was freaking out.

The others shouted words of encouragement. "You can do it!" Looking back, I now realise that this was probably a turning point. From the moment this boy, the toughest in our group, experienced the encouragement of the others at the moment when he felt weak, the dynamics of our group changed. Instead of their energy going into fighting one another and testing one another's strength, they began to work together.

I once had a teacher of educational philosophy who would leave the classroom in mid-sentence and re-enter having taken on the persona of a famous philosopher. It was always amusing, but it was also a great way to get us to use our imagination. Let us now imagine that Rousseau was also observing what happened that day on the banks of the Wisconsin River and allow him to enlighten us.

"You have forgotten there are two kinds of love. When you were trying to rationally explain why he should respect others, Justin only saw this as an attempt to control and frustrate him. This only added to the threat he had experienced in his childhood and his craving for dominance and prestige. This is what I refer to as *amour propre*. It displaced that other kind of passion, *amour de soi*, the innate concern to preserve one's own existence and to have a fruitful life. Justin will need *amour de soi* if he is to have the strength to become a successful agent in his own recovery from the trauma in his childhood."

Rousseau continues, "When Justin froze on the cliff, he experienced, in a helpful way, the real limits of his powers and abilities. At that moment when he was vulnerable, he was freely given encouragement and recognition from his peers without having to dispossess others."

It is not only kids growing up in inner city neighbourhoods that experience imminent, ongoing malice and threat. My meetings with Mairi continued. I learned that despite her cheeky smile and Glaswegian swagger, she was easily shamed. I knew some of the details about her early childhood. Over the next few weeks, I was to learn more.

Most of our conversations would begin by Mairi telling me about phone calls from her dad who was in prison. Something was weighing on her mind. I could imagine an unsuspecting teacher publicly reprimanding her and then being shocked and outraged when Mairi's anger erupted. I gave her time; I held back from giving advice or censoring her for her outbursts. The more I listened by expressing my curiosity and empathy, the more she shared and the more I understood her sense of shame and vulnerability.

"When I was little, my mum would lock me in a room when she was taking drugs. My mum and dad would fight. Sometimes one of my mum's friends would try to help me but she was a junkie as well."

I asked, "Have you ever felt like what happened to you was your own fault?"

I was taken back by the force of her answer.

"I always thought it was my fault."

Mairi told me she was worried about her dad coming out of prison. Her dad had been incarcerated because of what he had done to Mairi. Mairi told me she wanted to say to her dad that he would have to do better. I said, "I can't tell you exactly what to say, but you show a lot of courage to be honest about these things."

Next week Mairi continued, "I told him on the phone that this is his last chance to be a parent to me. If he gets it wrong this time, I am going to cut him off. I don't think he took me seriously; I asked my gran to tell him."

I commented: "It must have been really hard for you when you were little and your mum locked you in a room and your dad didn't help you." I wanted Mairi to experience my empathy at the time when she had felt most helpless and vulnerable. "Have you ever wondered if the anger you feel has something to do with what happened to you when you were little?"

"Most of it." Again, I was surprised by the force of her answer.

"Perhaps being angry was the only way you could protect yourself. Maybe you needed to feel stronger when other people were not protecting you?"

Mairi replied, "One boy was picking on me saying things. When he found out how angry I get, he stopped picking on me."

"So getting angry still helps you?"

"It helps me get out my stress. I cry when I am angry."

Finally, I ventured some advice, "Rather than say you have anger issues, wouldn't it be better to say you have issues with what happened to you when you were little?"

It would be naive to think Mairi will never be angry again, especially when she is publicly shamed or made to feel weak. The issues around her anger are not fully resolved, but fixing her anger was never my intention. If I had tried to *anger manage* her, Mairi would have believed her anger was her problem and she needed to fix it. I gave her time so that together we could explore her feelings and thoughts about what happened, and I commended her whenever she expressed courage. I prompted her to think about context, but I tried not impose my preconceived ideas. Where she was most vulnerable, I expressed empathy. I rarely had to prompt Mairi; she told me when she wanted to talk and when she had enough. Mairi's question: "Can we do something happier now?" was my cue to take out the game of UNO cards.

Mairi has a much better chance of realising that she doesn't need her anger anymore to protect herself. However, I think it is important to acknowledge that sometimes the anger young people struggle with can end in tragedy.

A couple of years ago, BBC news flashed up on my TV screen the name and photo of a young man instantly recognisable to me. He was one of the boys who canoed with me down the Wisconsin river. In fact, Juan was the one in the group that I thought had the best chance of recovering from the trauma of growing up in the inner city of Chicago. Although he had a problem with fighting other boys, I never felt threatened. Rather, he had made some good choices; he had sought out relationships with adults who could offer him support and love.

I listened to the details of another mass shooting. Juan had parked outside a hospital and shot a doctor, a pharmacist, a police officer, and then himself. There were triggering circumstances, broken relationships, and perhaps a tendency to be impulsive. But it was still hard to understand why. Here was a young man who had given up on life, and that is profoundly sad and shocking.

Caring for young people who suffer so deeply and sometimes cause great suffering in the lives of others raises deep and disturbing questions. How do these tragedies and the suffering of others affect us, and how can we continue to offer hopeful and sensitive care? I once asked a scientist working on a nuclear fusion project a question: "I bet it is hard to explain to someone like me what exactly you do?"

The scientist replied enthusiastically, "No, it's easy. My work is like 'balancing a pencil on its point.'"

Seriously, how do we keep a balance between wanting to give up because our work seems futile and seeking to control every bad thing that can happen to a young person? How do we not become indifferent to suffering on the one hand and also avoid becoming unrealistic in our sense of responsibility for the lives of others? Unresolved or unbalanced, we either give up, or we make people our projects. We end up struggling with anxiety and feeling frustrated by our lack of control.

I wonder if you have ever been in a situation like this? You have had an outstanding experience with a young person, and as they go home at the end of the day all you can think about is the chaos that the young person is going home to. Perhaps you have opened your home to a child and given them all the love you can give, but you know they are going back to a family where nothing much has changed. You agonise over your inability to really change things and end up asking "What's the point?" We need to recover the possibility of *acting well*, of doing the best we can in a given situation, whatever may become of it.[3] Ultimately our motivation to keep on acting well in the face of suffering and chaos will probably depend on our personal values and deeply held beliefs.

To those who prescribe simplistic solutions such as anger management, I recognise that there is a genuine desire to help. Having a solution helps us feel we know how to do our job, but there may be potentially harmful reasons for why we seek simple solutions to complex problems. Experiencing another person's anger and aggression can alter the way we think. When relating to young people who have experienced maltreatment and interpersonal trauma, our thinking can become focused solely on outcomes.[4] We find ourselves acting rather than thinking, making rigid assumptions about a young person rather than recognising the nuances of their behaviour and the uncertainty of our own thinking.

In addition, the very things that I want to change in you, if I am honest, I can probably recognise in my own life. For example, can we really say that road rage is different to another kind of aggression? Are we not all tempted to elevate our desire for recognition and respect to the point of aggressively putting others down? Based on his experiences of being imprisoned in the Soviet Gulag, Solzhenitsyn observed:

> If only there were evil people somewhere insidiously committing evil deeds, and it were necessary only to separate them from the rest of us and destroy them. But the line dividing good and evil cuts through the heart of every human being.[5]

If I am honest about my own tendencies, should I not approach a young person in a more gentle and non-judgmental way? Doing so, I probably have the best chance of being able to challenge how they see the world, especially when their view of the world has been distorted by suffering caused by others.

Keeping It Real

- Learn to be in the moment with young people when they are angry. Hold back from giving rational explanations and trying to fix their problems.
- When trying to understand the significance of their anger, listen for the clues. Pay attention to the context.
- Take time to explore the issues without judging the right and wrong of a situation or action.
- Don't be dismissive of the threat the young person is experiencing, real or perceived.
- Don't deal just with the consequences of anger. Remember anger has all kinds of causes.
- Don't underestimate the value of experiences where young people learn the limit of their power and ability to be in control, but make sure they are also able to learn what it is like to be supported and cared for when they feel vulnerable.
- Empathy is a powerful tool to help children re-imagine the possibilities in their lives.

References

1. Dent N. *A Rousseau Dictionary*. Oxford, UK: Blackwell; 1992.
2. Gilles V. Social and emotional pedagogies: critiquing the new orthodoxy of emotion in classroom behaviour management, *British Journal of Sociology of Education*. 2011; 32(2): 185-202.
3. O'Donovan O. *Begotten or Made?* Oxford, UK: Oxford University Press; 1984.

4. Bevington D, Fuggle P, Fonagy P, Target M, Asen E. Innovations in practice: Adolescent Mentalization-Based Integrative Therapy (AMBIT) – a new integrated approach to working with the most hard to reach adolescents with severe complex mental health needs. *Child and Adolescent Mental Health*. 2013; 18(1): 46 - 51. Available from: http://discovery.ucl.ac.uk/1385449/2/Fonagy_AMBIT_for_CAMH_finalSubmission.pdf [Accessed September, 2019].
5. Solzhenitsyn A. *The Gulag Archipelago 1918-1956: An Experiment in Literary Investigation* [e-book]. Harvill Press: London; 2003 [cited 22/10/2019].

10

"Change is Hard": A Personal Perspective

Why should we take a more humble and gentle approach to young people who struggle with anger? It seems counterintuitive and maybe even foolish. Firstly, I think it is important that we think about our own emotional state, especially when we are relating to young people whose behaviour can seem volatile, unpredictable, and threatening. In an ethnographic study of behaviour support units in three schools in London, Val Gillies observed an ironic incongruence between a curriculum designed to engender emotional skills and the emotionally fraught attitudes of many of the staff.

> School staff could feel overwhelmed by the frustration, anger, and irritation when engaging with persistent misbehaviour …." Gillies concludes: "This intense emotional connection to the work could make for an unconvincing arena in which to teach techniques of emotional restraint, as pupils themselves often recognised.[1]

A couple of years ago, I was asked to help a little boy (I will call him Frank) who struggled with anger issues. Each week, as soon as he saw me at the door of his classroom, he beamed with a smile that said, "Get me out of here!"

One day as we walked side by side looking for a room to meet, my little charge began to skip. Another teacher walking the opposite way asked him what he was doing. When he didn't immediately stop in his tracks, she looked furious, and demanded that he stop. Later I went to the head teacher and asked for a room to be assigned so that we didn't have to go looking and risk this kind of scrutiny.

I also tried my best to help Frank manage his anger. He often felt he was dealt with unfairly in the classroom, but I also had no doubt that this clever little guy could cause his teachers some considerable angst. My initial goal was to help him become more assertive and less aggressive.

A couple of weeks later, guess who comes into our little closet-like room? Yes, it is the teacher who doesn't like skipping. "What are you doing in here? You need to find somewhere else to work."

"No, we don't. We are staying here," I replied. She glared at me, turned and walked out.

I thought to myself, "I better make the best use of this situation." In an authoritative voice, I said to Frank, "You see that was a good example of what I meant when I was talking about being assertive."

Frank piped back, "Mr. Woodier, that wasn't assertive. That was rude."

Frank was probably right. I had best put that experience down to another failed attempt at anger management, but it also demonstrates what Gillies observed about "the emotionally charged nature of daily school life."[1] I think examples like this should also nudge us toward greater humility when we try to correct the problems we identify in other people's lives. As teachers, we expect a "highly regulated approach to emotions in the classroom,"[1] but at the same time we seem oblivious to how we regulate our own affect and the impact this has on our young people.

As a Christian, I have some compelling reasons for responding with greater humility toward others in their struggles and failures. I am conscious not only of my own failings but also my reticence in admitting my need for help. C.S. Lewis, observed in *Mere Christianity* that it is this area, pridefulness, that Christian morals differ most sharply from all other morals: "If anyone would like to acquire humility…the first step is to realise one is proud."[2]

This kind of humility also acknowledges that I am limited in my power to change others. My understanding of you is only at best partial, and this should make me at once open to the possibility that I am missing a piece of puzzle, and I need to listen to your view of things. Humility doesn't mean I lack passion or conviction. It doesn't mean that I think the truth is negotiable. Rather it is willing to recognise my own error and to bring my opinions into line with the truth. Thus, Christianity gives me insight into my limitations and fallibility and my appreciation of how difficult it can be to change attitudes and behaviours. My disposition towards others, even those who are struggling with anger, should be gentler.

Just last week, a teacher told me that one of his pupils said, "Anger management doesn't work. I have tried it and it doesn't help." The words of that young person sound like a plea for help, something like: "Show me how I can change!" Changing the character flaws we identify, or others identify in us, can only happen through our experience of grace, a relationship with someone who generously gives of themselves. It cannot flow from our own strength of character or by improving some aspect of our environment alone. I am not excusing apathy when it comes to acting on behalf of a child when that child is being harmed or maltreated. Only that we accept that changing circumstances alone is usually insufficient. It cannot change a disposition or free someone completely from their past. The yearning for self-transformation is of course nothing new. Augustine understood from personal experience the feelings of helplessness that confront us when faced with the task of real versus superficial change: "But by grace, not by nature."[2]

Examples of the transformative effects of grace abound in literature. For instance, consider Victor Hugo who develops this theme in *Les Miserables*. When Jean Valjean is escorted by the gendarmes to the Bishop's house, he expects nothing less than to be shamed and condemned for his crime of stealing the silver cutlery from this man who had shown him kindness. Instead, he receives a most unexpected challenge from the elderly Bishop:

"Ah! here you are!" he exclaimed, looking at Jean Valjean. "I am glad to see you. Well, but how is this? I gave you the candlesticks too, which are of silver like the rest, and for which you can certainly get two hundred francs. Why did you not carry them away with your forks and spoons?"

The Bishop drew near to him, and said in a low voice: "Do not forget, never forget, that you have promised to use this money in becoming an honest man."

Jean Valjean, who had no recollection of ever having promised anything, remained speechless. The Bishop resumed with solemnity: "Jean Valjean, my brother, you no longer belong to evil, but to good. It is your soul that I buy from you; I withdraw it from black thoughts and the spirit of perdition, and I give it to God."[3]

Grace is transformative because it is more than just a reprieve; it issues a challenge. The gift of silver from the Monseigneur provides Jean Valjean with the resources to change the course of his life. Generous self-giving, within a committed relationship, is probably the most potent force for personal transformation. Christians similarly are given the resources to respond to such a challenge through a relationship with Christ. Neither should other faithful and committed relationships be undervalued as the means through which lives can be transformed.[4]

I wonder how young people, especially those who struggle with anger, might respond to us if, like Monseigneur Bienvenu, we remembered that we too are similarly tempted to become impulsive or to use our anger to get our way. We might also heed Bienvenu's advice to condemn "nothing in haste and without taking circumstances into account" and to "examine the road over which the fault has passed."[3]

A young person I met this summer told me something about how hard his life had been; he had lived in multiple foster homes, and he had become so depressed he had tried to take his life. He didn't want to struggle with depression, but his comment to me was, "Change is hard!" I agree, but God's grace gives me reason to be optimistic in my response to young people who may have lost hope. The gift of what it means to be human, to be made in the image of God, carries with it a potential to be changed by the Giver. In the words of Oliver O'Donovan, there is a "good that makes good." It is in encountering the good, a personal relationship with God, that we experience the source of all good, and we are called to respond.

There are other young people I have known where it seems there is only tragedy. Juan's story and the shooting in that hospital car park in Chicago left me feeling profoundly conflicted. I didn't want to make him sound like a victim, but I couldn't ignore the reality of how hard his life had been growing up in the inner city. I struggled with how to reconcile what I remembered of him as a boy, and the image I saw of him on the TV screen and his portrayal as a perpetrator of carnage. I felt that by writing about this tragedy I was in some way using something that shouldn't be used.

I realised that actually we need to deal with the kinds of questions that Juan's actions, his life, and death, raise. We need to face our fears. What happens when what we do isn't enough? We also need to recognise how tragedy affects our motivation. How do we deal with the half-heartedness that creeps in after things don't go as we had hoped? If I don't deal with these questions, then unresolved issues become nagging doubts through which hope and optimism drain away. For me, Juan's story raises theological issues: questions about good and evil that I have no choice but to deal with if I want to share my life with children who have experienced abuse and neglect.

First, we must consider the perfectibility of humans. The Christian viewpoint is neither biased toward Locke nor Rousseau. It neither sees humans as completely good but corrupted by society nor vice versa. It doesn't allow us to be simplistic about the root cause of evil. Human beings, as described by Augustine, are corrupt by nature, carrying within each one of us a legacy of sin that debases even our affections and desires. Although we are not as bad as we could be, there is no part of me untouched by my deep-seated orientation away from God; there is no "island of righteousness."[5] My only hope of real transformative change comes from outside of me.

Augustine wrote: "Participating in his righteousness and immortality, (we) lose our own properties of sin and mortality, and preserve whatever good quality he had implanted in our nature, perfected now by sharing in the goodness of his nature."[6]

The Christian position on the potential of humans for good or evil is therefore both realistic and hopeful. Instead of a fatalistic attitude which would say we are defined by our past experiences, we are hopeful that through grace we can change. We realise that although perfection cannot be achieved in this world, our destiny need not be defined by what has happened to us. For the young person struggling with something like anger, there is the potential to resolve issues and to become more fully the person God intended.

This Christian understanding of good and evil must also be nuanced. Like Solzhenitsyn's awareness of his own tendency to act with malice even while experiencing the cruelty of his captors in a Gulag camp, the Christian understanding of good and evil takes the ground away from those who are tempted to simplistically divide the world into victims and perpetrators. Therefore, an appreciation of grace transforming my life, should create a humility that is incompatible with an attitude that looks down on or treats others harshly. The experience of grace, living in a transformative relationship with God, places a duty on Christians to act with humility toward those who have perpetrated evil on others.

Another issue that we need to have the courage to examine is the tendency to feel our work is futile. Can we really make a difference especially when we reflect back on how many young people seem to be trapped in lives of self-destruction which are not entirely of their own making? Here, too the Christian perspective offers real resources for hope.

This fear of giving myself to something that seems doomed to fail has caused me sometimes to hold back from unreservedly loving and caring for a person. I was reminded of the depth of conflicted emotion that comes with this dilemma through a recent conversation with a young person. She knew that I work with children who are looked after, and she told me that her parents were temporary foster carers for infants. She said, "I can't really love these babies, because I know they are going back to families where nothing has changed, and that breaks my heart."

Faced with the reality of how little influence or control I actually have over the futures of young people, I have searched intently for a perspective that would allow me to see how God can bring greater meaningfulness to actions that sometimes seem futile. This is an argument for a Christian ethic, a way of acting morally in a world that seems to be unresponsive to goodness. A world where evil seems to win and even the most vulnerable are not spared. Oliver O'Donovan, Anglican theologian, observes:

> One of the things that stops people from doing good is their vision of the world as depressing, closed down, tragedy ridden. A vision in which the world is hostile to human action. The resurrection of Jesus Christ teaches that God will not have it so, that God's world is restored to the goodness he intended for it and we are able to enter it, to engage in our action with it on that basis.[7]

Christians believe that God is free to act, creatively, powerfully, and graciously. I remember teaching a class of high schoolers about Easter. One boy, sat across from me, his head was down on the desk, as it always was when he was in my class. I ended the lesson with words something like, "If someone told me today that Jesus' bones had been discovered, I would close this Bible and never talk about Christ again." Very slowly for the first and last time in my class, that young man raised his head off the desk and looked at me. But the resurrection of Christ is not just a miracle that inspires Christians with a hope of life after death, as if that were not enough; it changes everything. In the words of O'Donovan, "In the resurrection we are taught to believe in God's will to restore the created world and humankind to its good purposes, the purposes for which it was made."[7]

However, the reality is that Christians live out this faith in the midst of a culture that has almost completely lost any awareness of the providence of God, his working out everything for his own ends. Instead of faith in a benevolent Creator, non-Christians and often Christians try ever harder to control the chaos that threatens to engulf. The Christian confession must acknowledge the limits to man's responsibility with regard to the future and trust more that God has a role for each individual in his overarching plan. O'Donovan encourages Christians to: "Recover the possibility of 'acting well,' of contributing to the course of events of a deed, which, whatever may become of it, is fashioned rightly in response to the reality that confronts the agents as he acts."[8]

What does this mean in practice? It means that I can act well and know that God has full liberty to use my acting well for his good purposes. I can think of at least two ways God used the good acts of others in my life to draw me to him.

I remember as a young boy reading CS Lewis' Narnia series, but I had no-one to help me understand the allegorical nature of the story. I remember thinking, "If there is someone like Aslan, I wish I could know him."

Many years later as a teenager when I was travelling in Nepal, I became quite ill. When I arrived at the hospital in Kathmandu, I was seen by an American doctor. He advised me to get some rest before returning to the UK, and he gave me the address of a house where there were people who would care for me.

For the next week, I was looked after in the house run by Youth with a Mission. I remember the feeling of relief that I was in a place with people I could trust. A couple of years later when I was at crisis point and again far away from home, I knew I could find help from Christians. It was the missionaries in a small town in the Andes that reached out to me. This time I listened more sensitively to what they were saying about Christ.

Was C.S. Lewis tempted to doubt that God would use his books like *The Lion, the Witch, and the Wardrobe*? Did that American doctor imagine that morning when he wrote an address on a piece of paper that it could have any greater significance in the life of a teenager wandering far away from home?

O'Donovan's analysis and my personal experiences convince me that I can give of myself to others because the cosmos is not chaotic, but it is governed by a good and all-powerful God who is not wasteful with the *good act*. When we treat others well, when we act selflessly, we can create a space, an expectation, or a plausibility that there is a good Creator God who is personally able to redeem us and give our lives meaning.

I was reading *The Lion, the Witch, and the Wardrobe* with one of my pupils recently. I tentatively asked, "Does Aslan remind you of somebody? Somebody who is good and very powerful."

With a mischievous smile, my pupil replied, "Scooby Doo?" We both laughed. There wasn't much I could do to follow that!

I want to acknowledge the commitment of many non-Christian friends who give their unconditional love to young people, but I also want to point to what I think Christians have as a solid ground for sustained, committed, and loving relationships, even when those relationships sometimes end in tragedy or disappointment.

Addendum

As I review these chapters, I can see a potential source of conflict. I can hear the voice of a teacher saying something like, "But he needs to take responsibility for what his actions." These kinds of comments are asking us questions about the meaning and limits of agency. If, as your read this book, you feel that sense of conflict, you are probably right, because I write a lot more on my own agency than I do about the agency of my pupils. In order to act well, young people need to be reassured that they are not held prisoner by their past, or their future. They need to be shown that their world is benevolent and not devoid of values and good. They can't do that on their own.

References

1. Gilles V. Social and emotional pedagogies: critiquing the new orthodoxy of emotion in classroom behaviour management, *British Journal of Sociology of Education*. 2011; 32(2): 185-202.
2. Lewis C. S. *Mere Christianity,* London: Fount Paperbacks; 1977.
3. Hugo V. *Les Misérables: Complete in Five Volumes* Translator: Isabel F. Hapgood Available from: www.gutenberg.org/files/135/135-h/135-h.htm#link2HCH0003 [Accessed 4 November, 2019].
4. Grudem W. *Systematic Theology*. Leicester, UK: Inter Varsity Press; 1994.
5. Sproul R.C. The Pelagian captivity of the soul. *Modern Reformation*. 2001: 10(3): 22-29. Available from: https://www.bible-researcher.com/sproul1.html [Accessed 4 November, 2019].
6. Augustine. *The City of God*. Trans. Marcus Dods. NY: The Modern Library; 2000.
7. O'Donovan O. What is the point of the cross of Jesus? Oliver O'Donovan at The Veritas Forum Available from: **https://www.youtube.com/watch?v=L4BKvj8AI4c** [Accessed 19 February, 2020].
8. O'Donovan O. *Begotten or made?* Oxford, UK: Oxford University Press; 1984.

Part III
Asking to Understand and Being Curious About the Inner Life

11

Verbs of the Heart: Understanding Why We Do the Things We Do

Half a dozen professionals sit around the table; they look wearily at one another. The head teacher asks, "Tell us about your work with Johnny." We talk about our concerns; his behaviours begin to stack up. Johnny did this and then he did that.

The plan up to this point has been largely to keep adding professionals: a teaching assistant, a school counsellor, a mentor. (It reminds me of how I cook; I keep throwing ingredients into the pot hoping something good will come out in the end, but it rarely does). We have been here before and things keep getting worse. Each plan fails, and I sense that the agenda of the meeting is shifting. This is not about Johnny or finding a plan anymore. It is about building a consensus: he shouldn't be in a mainstream school. It is as if collectively we have given up hope of change.

His behaviours are telling us something, but we need to think differently about the kind of support we are providing and how we are functioning as a group of professionals.

I am itching to ask a question: "If we don't understand why Johnny is behaving that way, then isn't it possible the things we think are helping could be making it worse? Johnny finds it difficult to feel securely attached to one adult, let alone to all these strangers who are trying to reach out to him."

Finally, I get up the courage to ask, "Does anyone have an idea why he does that?"

His teacher replies, "I'm not a psychologist."

I admit that at first I wasn't sure why this teacher was unwilling to engage in this kind of reflective thinking about a young person's behaviours and underlying intentions. Was it her response to being called upon to talk about something for which she was unprepared? Alternatively, was it driven by her concern of who would be left holding responsibility when none of the interventions were working. Such a fear might be a powerful (even if it is unstated) concern in many of our professionals' meetings. There is possibly another more sinister reason, but I have never seen it acknowledged. Are we unconsciously distancing ourselves from a young person so that in the end it becomes easier to exclude them? We need to be ever so aware of our human tendency to dehumanize others when we perceive them as a threat. Sometimes the sense of threat is exacerbated by our lack of being in control.

As educators, we may be inclined to put the task of understanding behaviour out of reach of some of those who are best placed to support young people. The reality is that even training often falls short and expertise has its limits. I remember in my teacher training being taught how to carry out a Functional Behavioural Assessment and only later coming to realise for some young people almost anything could be an antecedent or trigger. The task of trying to connect so-called internal triggers to the consequences of their behaviour seemed both insurmountable and reductionist. Human beings and their complex behaviours cannot be adequately described in terms of the relationship between a stimulus and response.

As I reflected again on the school meeting, I could see the value of a more cautious approach. We should be prudent in how we understand other people's intentions. We should be aware of our tendency to believe we understand another person too well. Psychologists observe that parents who are good at understanding their child's mental states are also respectful of the opacity of other people's minds. There is a form of intrusive mentalizing that can take place, where separateness of minds is not respected and adults may feel too strongly that they understand what a child is thinking and feeling.[1]

I remember interviewing a young person who was care experienced. He identified a time in his primary school, where in his own words, "Things started to improve when I was in Mrs Jones' class."

"What was it that changed and helped things get better?" I asked.

"My teacher tried to understand me," was his straightforward answer.

It helps children develop secure attachments when they experience someone who tries to sensitively understand. And, in turn, their own capacity to reflect on and to understand other people's intentions grows. This imaginative and reflective capacity is surely one of the most basic human traits.

It is true we can't see directly into someone else's mind, but we can make an intelligent enquiry. The ability to understand interpersonal behaviour in terms of our own and others' mental states—such as desires, beliefs, goals, and feelings—is fundamental to what it means to be human.[1]

It makes sense that those who spend the most time with a young person probably have the most insight, but this sensitive work of taking a young person's perspective is not straightforward. Helping those adults closest to a young person sustain those connections has to be clearly defined and supported by other adults. It works best when we help each other mentalize.[2]

AMBIT (Adaptive Mentalization-Based Integrative Treatment) is an example of a programme that has developed a team approach to mentalizing.[3] It recognises first that our capacity to reflect on a young person's feelings and thoughts can be compromised by the fear and despair that comes when we connect to others and their pain. Similarly, it is realistic about the dynamics of a group of professionals with different goals who may doubt and misjudge one another. AMBIT uses a four-step process called *thinking together* that enables the key adult to be heard.[4] Their predicament (often some fear or worry) is empathised with and given clarity of meaning. The result is that the key adult is in a much better position to take up that curious, empathetic, and accepting stance.

Using the verbs of relationships

The structure of language itself may provide clues to understanding motives and intentions that otherwise are hard to identify. In the following questions, many of the verbs signify how a person relates to others; we can think of these as verbs of the heart. There is something mysterious and enigmatic about the heart when it refers to a person's inner self or psychological centre. It is where thinking, feelings, and will connect. It is where we often want to communicate to and where we want to see change. When a person opens their heart to another person, we find the essence of human relationship. However, it can also be a dark place of self-deception and self-condemnation.

Rather than asking the following questions directly (adapted from David Powlison's "X-Ray Questions"), keep them in mind as you observe and get to know a young person. Listen to how others experience a young person and compare your observations. We can use these kinds of questions to dissect the details of one particular incident or to help us think about patterns that characterise a young person's life.[5]

The answers can function as windows into another person's unique worldview. For example, one of the ways a child who has suffered maltreatment may stand out is by her difficulty expressing reciprocity toward others. Rather than looking outwardly to others to love and care for her, she may feel driven to avoid or to control others.

Don't be surprised if some of the answers to these questions are also counterintuitive, for example; the child may find the interest of an adult more of a threat than a comfort, and a young person may find safety in sabotaging a good experience or a promising relationship.

1. What does she love? What lights up her world? What gives her delight?

2. What does he desire, long for, wish? Do other people's desires rule over him? Whom does he feel he must please? Whose opinion counts?

3. What feeling is she trying to avoid? Is there something she hates?

4. What does he hope for? Where does he bank his hopes? Have his hopes been dashed?

5. What does she fear? What does she fear losing? What does she feel threatened by?

6. Where does he find refuge, safety, comfort, or escape? When fearful, discouraged, and upset where does he turn? Who can make it safe or better?

7. What or whom does she trust? In whose presence does she find her sense of well-being? Whose promises does she trust?

8. What beliefs does he hold about life, himself, others? What are his specific beliefs about his present situation?

Keeping It Real by Redefining the Task

How a young person relates to others is probably the most significant factor in understanding why he or she does the things they do. We use others to help us find meaning, identity, and self-understanding. Thinking about what a young person's behaviour is communicating allows an adult to approach that young person in a far more nuanced and sensitive way.

Instead of pushing more people into a young person's life, the task of the professionals around the table can shift to helping one or two key adults to understand and relate to a young person who otherwise may find change very difficult. When my thinking becomes more rigid and judgmental toward a young person, I need others to remind me what is unique and likeable about this child and to help me recover my empathy toward them. I have a proposal: What about redefining the task from how do we change this child's behaviour to how do we understand them and how do we help them know we are trying to understand them?

References

1. Fonagy P, Allison E. What is mentalization? In Midgley N, Vrouva I. (eds.) Minding the child. Hove: Routledge; 2012. p.11-34. 1. Fonagy P, Allison E. What is mentalization? In Midgley N, Vrouva I. (eds.) Minding the child. Hove: Routledge; 2012. p.11-34.

2. Bevington D, Fuggle P, Fonagy P. Applying attachment theory to effective practice with hard-to-reach youth: the AMBIT approach. *Attachment and Human Development.* 2015; 17(2): 1-18.

3. Bevington D. Working as therapists and allied professions with hard to reach youth. Interview with European Society of Child and Adolescent Psychiatry. 2019. Available from: https://www.escap.eu/care/teams-as-the-critical-agents-of-change-in-systems/

4. Anna Freud National Centre for Children and Families. Thinking Together. Available from: https://manuals.annafreud.org/ambit-static/thinking-together

5. Powlison D. X-ray questions: drawing out whys and wherefores of human behaviour. *JBC.* 1999; 18(1): 2-9.

12

They Call Me 'Trouble': The Peril of Not Repairing Relationships

Yet if he [Bruce] should give up what he has begun, and agree to make us or our kingdom subject to the King of England or the English, we should exert ourselves at once to drive him out as our enemy and a subverter of his own rights and ours …

This year marks the seven hundredth anniversary of Scotland's most famous letter. The declaration of Arbroath was sent on behalf of the Scottish barons to Pope John in Avignon. It gives us insight into one of the earliest examples of a contractual monarchy.[1] In other words, Robert the Bruce's claim to be king was only as strong as his commitment to protect the Scottish people. Since then, the notion of utility has inculcated most of our institutions. For example, often the assumption made in schools is that my right to belong to this community is only as good as my performance and my contribution to a common good. But where does that leave vulnerable young people whose behaviour in school is routinely seen as detrimental to others? We may need a radical shift in our thinking, if we are to find a basis for a more relational approach. Nowhere is this more acutely demonstrated than in how we repair relationships.

When I arrived in Michael's class, I could see his teacher was obviously upset. Michael was characteristically impulsive, found it hard to focus, and he took risks without any thought to his own safety. He was small for his age and had been diagnosed with fetal alcohol spectrum disorder. Once I got him out of the classroom, I could see I wasn't dealing with a defiant kid, but with a boy who just didn't know how to get things right most of the time.

"Michael, could you say sorry to your teacher if I go with you?" He nodded and we rehearsed what to say.

We tentatively approached the teacher, and I spoke first, "Michael has something to say."

"I'm sorry miss," Michael's voice was barely audible. There was a moment of silent anticipation, as we waited for her reply.

"I hope you mean it." Her words sounded menacing.

Instantly, Michael's head dropped. He looked like an inflatable toy suddenly punctured. I put my hand on his shoulder and guided him out of the classroom.

"That took some courage," I said but my words sounded hollow. Had I set up Michael to fail? I had assumed that his teacher, although stressed and weary, would accept an apology from a little boy. But I hadn't checked in with her to see how she was feeling. I learned that day that even adults need time to work things through. It is not always easy to act with compassion, and offering forgiveness carries some risk: What will I do if the same thing happens again? Will others see this as a weakness and take advantage of me? It is hard to sustain personal values when I feel like the institution I am part of defines my competence as a teacher by how well my children perform and my class behaves.

As much as we believe in the value of a relational approach, success can be impeded by our fear of losing control, of disorder, and of being judged incompetent and weak. We need a frame of reference, a set of values, that gives us common ground and helps us understand why and how to repair relationships. This framework should take into account unique aspects of how children develop; children are not just small adults. In addition, how we repair relationships and seek and offer forgiveness will depend on how we see ourselves functioning as a community. We need to consider what kinds of obligations we have toward one another and how those can bind us together and bring a sense of belonging.

I have learned from first-hand experience that repairing relationships requires a shift in my thinking which also leads to a significant change in relationship:

Nicola came out of class with some work from her teacher. In a demanding tone, she asked me to draw an illustration. Nicola is a good artist, and I thought she was being lazy, but when I declined to help, her whole demeanour changed. She frowned, snapped the pencil, ripped the paper, and stormed back into class.

For a moment, I thought, "No skin off my back, I'll just move on to the next class." But something held me. I sheepishly approached the classroom teacher, "Could you tell Nicola I will wait for her?"

The teacher looked at me and it felt as though I could read her mind: *You are meant to be the expert and even you can't manage her behaviour.*

I waited five minutes and Nicola reappeared. I used those five minutes to think through my response and find some composure.

"Nicola, I got that wrong today. When you came out to see me, you were smiling and chatting." My voice became more animated as I continued: "I thought to myself, 'This is just like any other day. You are in a good mood and we can chat.' But I see now I got that wrong." My expression changed and my voice was quieter and more plaintive. "I'm sorry."

Nicola dropped her head into her hands. "My gran said she is going to sell my Xbox today, because I wouldn't get out of bed."

Before you judge Nicola, you should know that she has very few possessions and even fewer friends. She lives with her disabled gran, and she is bullied because she wears old clothes that smell of cat pee.

I paused and replied with empathy, "That must be really hard. I know your Xbox means a lot to you." I didn't offer advice or challenge her. We began to work together, sitting side by side. I drew the outline of a picture and she added details to it. There was a completely different emotional tone between us. In fact, I can mark an enduring change in our relationship from that morning.

Since then, Nicola has been more open about her needs and more trusting of me to help her, and yet I nearly missed that opportunity. When she stormed off, my first reaction was to be annoyed and then embarrassed. I felt disrespected and I wanted people to see that she was to blame. I wanted to justify myself, but I had misattributed her intentions. Her behaviour wasn't personal. It would have been so easy to walk away and nurse my wounded pride and save some face.

If we slow down that encounter and examine it frame by frame, what actually happened?

- First, there was a shift in my thinking from, "I feel wronged, and I need to justify myself," to, "She is the child and I'm the adult, and I should take the initiative and show compassion," and, "This relationship matters more right now than what another teacher thinks about me."

- There was a moment of risk for me. Nicola could easily have chosen not to come back, and then I would have looked even more incompetent and felt more powerless, but I had a hunch that actually she wanted things to be fixed between us, and I was willing to take that risk.

- There was an unconditionality in my apology. I wasn't saying sorry because I wanted her to like me, and it wasn't, "I'm sorry, if you are sorry." I didn't attempt to correct or challenge her. It was her time to talk and my time to listen. She needed her experience of wrongdoing validated even if I wasn't the primary cause.

- I carefully matched her expressed affect, especially her sense of outrage at losing her Xbox. This game was one of the only ways she connected to her peers, and it was a really big deal to her. I needed to think what it is like to be a teenager in <u>her</u> world. Compassion opened a way for me to experience empathy, and that helped restore our connection.

Looking at how children need adults to help them repair relationships shows how powerful these kinds of encounters can be. Ed Tronick, Professor of Psychology at University of Massachusetts, has studied in minute detail how mothers (caregivers) and infants attune to one another. His conclusion is somewhat startling. Mother and infant interaction is not characterised by a perfect synchrony. Most of the time there is mismatching and interactive repair.

Mother and infant do not dance like Fred Astaire and Ginger Rogers, but rather dance in and out of loving attunement. When most of us dance, we bump into one another, apologise, and then get back to dancing together. The dancing is messy. Finding loving attunement again—the reparation of misattunements—builds love and trust; reparatory failure builds insecurity and distrust.[2]

In other words, this messy kind of dance is normal. "Reparation … is the social-interactive mechanism that drives and modifies infants' development."[2] It may be something we do as adults with infants without even being conscious of what we are doing, but when it comes to teenagers we seem to have forgotten how to dance.

The rupture and repair of relationships allows children to learn at a deep level who they are by how they are understood by an adult.[3] They also learn that adults can be reliable and trustworthy, and that there are ways of communicating that can resolve interpersonal difficulties. Children may gain confidence that enables them to approach new situations being hopeful about the stability of future relationships.

However, the how and why of repairing relationships raises questions that go beyond a purely developmental or therapeutic perspective. There are moral concerns at work here: people ask questions about a young person's moral responsibility and about the impact of a young person's behaviours on the wider community. We may be on a slippery slope if we bypass the importance of our collective moral conscience, but at the same time we need to consider the consequences of not repairing relationships.

At the beginning of this article, I referred to the way utility is used in society to bring cohesion: schools believe that individuals find a sense of belonging by working together toward a common good. In Scottish education, the common good is defined broadly by eight indicators of wellbeing: safety, health, achieving, nurtured, active, respected, responsible, and included.[4] Some of those indicators, like respect and responsibility, may sound aspirational, but can they transform behaviour? Such a vision runs into difficulties when young people believe that their right to belong in community is based primarily on their performance.

I spent a week talking to young people who were care experienced about their perceptions of belonging in school and their experiences of relational rupture and repair. I was genuinely surprised by some of their comments:

1. Have you ever felt like you don't belong in this school or in your class? What made you feel that way?

Pupil A. When the head teacher gets me, I am always in trouble. It's never nice. I am not wanted in this school. He wants me away and to never come back. He is nice to parents, but when I was younger, he grabbed my phone. All the time he says the teachers are sick of me. He isn't mean to everyone.

Pupil B. Uhuh. I just didn't fit in. I was angry.

Is this something you think about quite a lot?

B: Yes. I think about it. Depute [deputy] head teachers don't like me. My pupil support teacher hates me.

2. Do you feel that teachers like you? What kind of children do teacher's like?

A: The ones that behave and if teachers know you are trying. *He points at three children from his class.* She talks to them more. They stay out of trouble.

B: No. *Pause.* A lot of girl teachers like me. My nickname with teachers is 'Trouble.' *He pauses again.* They would say they like me, but they don't mean it.

3. Has a teacher ever said sorry to you? Have they ever said they treat you wrongly?

A: In primary school, I got blamed for starting a fight and I was kept in. It wasn't me. The teacher came back and apologized. I still didn't like her; she was crabbit. *Scots for ill-tempered.*

B: No. *Long pause.* I got in trouble, but it wasn't me and she said sorry. I was always in trouble in primary school. Teachers ought to be able to say things like that [say sorry].

4. If I came to you and said I was sorry because I had treated you wrongly …

A: *He interrupted me before I can finish the question.* I would forgive you. *I had not used the word 'forgiveness' in our conversation.*

B: *Again. I was interrupted before I could finish.* Would I be friendly with you? Yes. *He paused and smiled.* Because you take me away from classes I don't like.

The words of the young people speak for themselves, but something that isn't apparent is the emotion that came across in their conversations with me. Some sounded outraged, while others came across as more matter of fact or resigned to their situation. I was listening to young people who felt betrayed. Somewhere deep down, they still had the expectation that schools should be places where they are accepted and cared for. I wondered if there was some implicit promise they believed was not being honoured. If my hunch is correct, we may be raising a generation of young people who feel that the very institutions designed for their benefit actually serve someone else's agenda.

Is there a way to build an institution, like a school, where there is a strong ethos of inclusion, shared life, and common purpose? The way a parent and very young child learn to relate to one another may provide a blueprint. In the relationship between mother and child, one of the parties has greater authority and power and yet they are bound together not by a common interest but by compassion, and ultimately by the character and fidelity of the promise-maker. "I will meet your needs even if it means I am up every night," is the kind of promise we make to young children and sometimes our teenagers.

It is in the security of this committed relationship that children learn to assert themselves and to yield. The child asserts his need and wants to be in control but also learns to submit to his mother, trusting her to make him feel safe and secure. This dual capacity goes on to produce health and constancy in relationships.[5] In this archetypal relationship, there is a covenant, a binding mutual bond, based on certain promises, that appeals to fidelity, and includes provision for repair and forgiveness.

Fundamentally, covenanting does not look at others as a means to an end. The child learns that it is okay for mum to have a life of her own; he can exist without her constant attention. Similarly, the child must learn that he does not exist to make his parents feel better about themselves. Think about how this contrasts to the kinds of relationship many young people have with their school, when it is not clear whose interests are really at the core of our institutions.

I am probably raising more questions than I have answered. There is still the pragmatic what-to-do-in the-moment to be addressed. "How do we respond when Paul sets off the fire alarm for the third time this week?" As with any committed relationship, there are responsibilities and commitments expected of both parties. It is not just one way. However, ask yourself first "Is there an opportunity to repair this relationship in such a way that reinforces my fidelity as a leader? Can this be turned around to invite a young person to trust in the integrity of this relationship and the institution?"

Institutions work relationally by:

- Recognizing the fundamental importance of the promises they make, some formal and declared, but others implicit and lived-out.
- Having leaders who champion those promises and values; for example, showing compassion.
- Consistently seeking opportunities for repair and forgiveness, when relationships are ruptured.
- Appealing to fidelity and trust rather than coercing and shaming others.
- Seeking transformational change: Repairing relationships allows us to understand who we are at a deeper level because we see our value through how the other person sees us and their commitment to the relationship.
- Recognizing what we have in common, especially those special times of joy and sorrow in a community.
- Moving towards others in truth and love.

If you find yourself becoming cynical at this point, consider where your doubts are coming from. Theologian Walter Brueggemann, commenting on how communities can be transformed, warns us:

> We have grown so accustomed to the ways in which institutions are self-serving, in which every institution serves primarily its functionaries in order to preserve jobs and enhance personal well-being. This is true of government, court, school, hospital, church. Because the forms of public life are so complex, we despair of change. We expect ourselves and certainly others to be exploited. And we do not imagine it can be otherwise.[6]

Not long after I moved from the States and started teaching in Glasgow, I observed an event, and its memory still brings a smile to my face. One morning in January, I was handed a piece of tartan fabric to pin on my jacket and asked to prepare for a Burn's Night celebration. The whole school was invited, even one ten-year-old who was renowned for fighting and spent more time in the head teacher's office than any other child. Imagine my surprise when the music began and our stalwart head teacher partnered with this little boy. They danced with gusto, their steps and movement in synchrony. For a short time, it seemed that all rivalries, grievances, and even coolness were cast aside: everyone joined together to celebrate their identity, their Scottish-ness.

I am not naïvely suggesting that all our problems can be solved by an event, but a dance may be worth more than a thousand words. Young people need to see compassion and integrity in the adults who teach and care for them. A leader who authentically demonstrates those values broadcasts a message to staff and students about what that school stands for. Our commitment to find what we have in common, to repair relationships, and to offer forgiveness must be foundational to how we build schools that nurture a morality that does not measure a person's value and dignity based on their utility or how much they contribute to society. If we get this wrong, we risk raising a generation whose sense of betrayal by those who should care for them will permeate every aspect of their public lives.

Keeping it Real

- Are you able to stand back from the situation and shift your view towards a more compassionate one? Noticing something about a young person that reminds you he or she is still a child might help you feel more protective towards them.
- If you have the role of leader of an institution, how will you demonstrate your personal commitment to those young people who are disenfranchised, and who tend to doubt they are wanted or belong in school?
- Are you taking the initiative in restoring relationships? Showing compassion and humility doesn't make you look weak or incompetent. Think of the reward of helping a child learn to trust an adult more deeply.
- Are you celebrating what it means to belong to a community? Use special occasions and other tangible reminders to reinforce and reflect on that commitment to one another: lunch with a tutor group, welcoming a new pupil, and saying goodbye to someone who is leaving. Be especially watchful that special occasions don't also exclude the very young people we want to reach.

References:

1. Scotland's History: The Declaration of Arbroath. BBC. Available from: http://www.bbc.co.uk/scotland/history/articles/declaration_of_arbroath/
2. Tronick E. The caregiver–infant dyad as a buffer or transducer of resource enhancing or depleting factors that shape psychobiological development. Australian and New Zealand Journal of Family Therapy. 2017; 38: 561–572.
3. Fonagy P. Mutual regulation, mentalization and therapeutic action: A reflection on the contributions of Ed Tronick to developmental and psychotherapeutic thinking. Psychoanalytical Inquiry. 2015; 35(4): 355-369.
4. Scottish Government. Getting It Right for Every Child (GIRFEC). Available from: https://www.gov.scot/policies/girfec/wellbeing-indicators-shanarri/
5. Brueggemann, W. The Covenanted Self: Explorations in Law and Covenant. 1999; Minneapolis: Fortress Press.
6. Brueggemann W. Covenant as a subversive paradigm. Christian Century. 1980: 1094-1099. Available from: https://www.religion-online.org/article/covenant-as-a-subversive-paradigm/

13

Emotionally Protecting Children Allows Them to Express Who They Really Are

"I thought 'e was going to hit me"

Children who have been maltreated often find it hard to express who they really are without making themselves more vulnerable. School is a place where they are particularly at risk, but it is also a place where the curriculum may give them opportunities to understand their inner lives and experience the interest and concern of others.

I once worked with a boy who was adopted. At the beginning of his first year in high school, he was asked by his teacher to write about his family. He raised his hand and asked, "Which family?" After that he was bullied by some of his classmates.

On the other hand, much of children's literature is rich in themes and characters that can provide opportunities for young people to learn about their inner lives. Heather Geddes writes that, "The task itself can be a bridge which links the teacher and pupil. Across this bridge, the pupil experiences reliable interest and concern without feeling threatened by overwhelming feelings."[2] Using stories as that kind of bridge can be especially beneficial for children with attachment difficulties who are resistant to intimacy in relationships.

Harry was ten years old. His mum had died of a drug overdose, and he lived with a family member. He called her "Mum," but his teachers were concerned that his "mum" leaned on Harry for her emotional needs. Harry had a lot of reasons to be sad and to question if anyone loved him. The only emotion he seemed able to express was anger, which was often directed at his teachers.

I thought of Harry as being like one of those Pre-Renaissance paintings. There was very little perspective, very little depth to his self-expression. He seemed to appear only in two dimensions. Like other children who have suffered maltreatment, he was preoccupied with how others evaluated him.[3]

When I arrived at his school, I found Harry sitting in the head teacher's office. There had been an altercation during break.

As we walked down the corridor I asked, "You were in the head teacher's office. Was anything wrong?"

"No. She was asking me questions about what some other boys were doing."

Harry was very guarded about talking about anything he perceived might make him look bad. Each week I tried to catch him a little off guard, "So how are you doing?"

"Good."

Harry always said, "good," even when things were obviously not going well.

Occasionally, children like Harry talk about themselves in a way that opens up a depth of insight and emotion. When this happens in school, it can make them vulnerable, especially when they do this in front of their classmates. We need to be prepared so that we can give them a safe way to express themselves.

Harry's class were reading *Goodnight Mister Tom*, the story of Willie, a ten-year-old evacuee, who is abused by his mother but finds unconditional love when he moves to live with an older man in the country. Harry and I read sections of dialogue together and recorded them to make an audio book. Harry liked this. He laughed at my attempt at Mister Tom's accent, and I laughed at his attempt at a London accent. Dialogue seemed to bring us closer together.

We listened to the recording, but I was not happy. "There is too much of my voice," I said. "I would like to begin the recording with you speaking. You could voice Willie's thoughts as he thinks about his first day with Mister Tom."

Harry replied, "I can't do that. I don't know what he would think."

I prompted him, "Do you remember that Willie thought Mister Tom was going to hit him?"

Harry began to talk as if he was Willie. He put on his best London accent. "I thought 'e was going to hit me, but 'e didn't. He just picked up that stick to poke the fire."

I began to type. Harry looked at the words and said, "No, he doesn't sound like that."

"You're right. I'll take the 'h' off the beginning of the words that begin with 'h'. How does Mister Tom show he cares for Willie?" I asked Harry.

"He bought him clothes. He took care of him when he fainted."

Harry read over the script again, and then, without prompting, he added, "I like this place better than my 'ouse. I've got me own bed. I think Mister Tom is going to 'elp me. Maybe this is what it's like to be loved."

Harry said the words with such expression, I couldn't help but think he was speaking from a more personal understanding of Willie's character. He was no longer trying to present an image of himself; there was something more real and more three-dimensional about him.

I commented, "You said that just the way I think Willie would have said it." Harry smiled.

I didn't take the conversation any further. My purpose was not to get Harry to talk about his own experience of neglect or abuse. It was enough that he was able to express something of his true self, and he experienced my interest and curiosity without feeling I had intruded on his inner world.

"If you want to speak to troubled children you are far more likely to be successful if you do it through 'their' language- the language of image, metaphor or story."[4]

Keeping it Real

Parents and carers:

Talk to your child or young person about how to answer questions their peers may ask or questions that may come up in class: "Who was that lady that picked you up from school?" "Why did you move here?" Help them be discerning about who they talk to and what to disclose to their friends and in public.

Teachers:

- Be careful about how you introduce activities. Try to anticipate questions that might make a young person vulnerable. Instead of just saying, "Write about your family," add, "If you are adopted or have lived with more than one family, you might want to write about the family you live with now. Also, if you live some of the time with your mum and some of the time with your dad, you can choose which family to write about." In that way you can also normalise young people's experiences by recognising the variety of family backgrounds.
- If you are planning class discussion, speak privately, beforehand to a young person who may be more sensitive and reassure them that you won't call on them to answer unless they volunteer first.
- Identify the themes in literature that can inspire trust and hope, e.g. the role of the 'rescuer' or trust between characters.
- For the pupil who finds it difficult to even talk about the feelings of characters in a book, allow them to simply listen in to the answers from young people who are more confident.
- Where there is a risk that the content of a lesson may resonate with a young person's traumatic life experience, build time into the lesson so there is a chance for a young person to regain their equilibrium before they leave your classroom or move on to another activity.

References

1. Killick S, Thomas T. *Telling Tales: Storytelling as Emotional Literacy*. Blackburn, UK: Educational Printing Services Ltd.; 2007.
2. Geddes H. *Attachment in the Classroom: The Links Between Children's Early Experience, Emotional Well-Being and Performance in School*. London: Worth Publishing; 2006.

3. Tangney J P. Dearing R L. *Shame and Guilt*. New York: The Guilford Press; 2002.
4. Sunderland M. *Using Storytelling as a Therapeutic Tool with Children*. Milton Keynes: Speechmark Publishing; 2000.

Additional Reading

Golding K. *Using Stories to Build Bridges with Traumatized Children: Creative Ideas for Therapy, Life Story Work, Direct Work and Parenting*. London: Jessica Kingsley Publishers; 2014.

Killick S, Boffey M. *Building Relationships Through Storytelling: A Foster Carer's Guide to Attachment and Stories*. The Fostering Network. Available from:
https://www.thefosteringnetwork.org.uk/sites/www.fostering.net/files/content/building-relationships-through-storytelling-31-10-12.pdf_[Accessed 11-5-17]

14

Understanding Attachment Helps Teachers Build Resilience in Young People

Resilience can be one of those buzz words in education. It is easy to talk about, but trying to help vulnerable young people become more resilient can be more difficult than we imagine.

You present a young person with a once in a lifetime opportunity, for example, an outward-bound course. However, when the day comes and the bus is ready to leave, he is nowhere to be found.

You worked all year to prepare your class for the transition to high school. One of your pupils, from a difficult home situation, refuses to attend the new school after the first week.

Is it possible that we underestimate the vulnerability of some children because we don't get how profoundly trauma* impacts young people? In addition, our view of resilience is so culturally conditioned that we think of resilience too much in terms of an individual's strengths, rather than recognising the importance of the relationships that surround a young person. A stand-on-your-own-two-feet, individualistic notion of resilience may be very unhelpful.

A recent phone call to a foster parent reminded me that in many cases building resilience in young people does not go to plan. Several years ago, I began a piece of work with a high schooler, David. I carefully planned the activities based on what I understood about resilience, but I missed the importance of long-term relationships.

David's teachers in high school were pulling their hair out. He was restless in class, found it difficult to focus, and often acted like a clown. During my first meeting with him, I quickly realised here was a young man who wasn't going to sit and listen to me. We needed to do something active together. After playing badminton with him several times, I could see another side to him. Behind his constant fidgeting and impish grin, he was kind, gentle, and eager to please. I began to think about how I could use my relationship with him to help him reintegrate into his school. He needed an opportunity to experience real success in something that he saw as being worthwhile. He needed a challenge; I needed to stop losing at badminton.

Risk, resilience, and attachment

Education can have a positive impact on resiliency. For example, schools provide opportunities for children to achieve a sense of mastery, the feeling that comes from doing something well. Young people also have the opportunity to explore different social roles that can help them build a more pro-social identity.[1] However, for young people like David, school often reminds them of failure, and they too easily become cast in the role of a troublemaker.

David was at risk long before he started school. He was probably exposed to alcohol while in his mother's womb. When we add up all of the risk factors in a young person's life things may look pretty bleak, but even then we can underestimate a young person's vulnerability. We don't realise that risk factors interact in a way that is not just a simple one plus one. A risk factor such as an insecure attachment can have a disproportionate influence on how a child is impacted by other traumatic experiences.[2,3] To some degree, all children are vulnerable; they all need adults that can help restore a sense of safety and control in a sometimes chaotic world. In this way, a secure attachment between child and caregiver mitigates the effects of trauma. However, the opposite is also true. A child who is insecurely attached may be more easily overwhelmed and unable to develop some of the core competencies, such as the capacity to self-regulate emotional states, that will help protect him against future adversity.[4]

The cascading effects of a child's early attachment experiences may explain why some young people are knocked back so hard by the stress, for example, of moving to a new school. They are like the house built on sand.

Resilience can be defined as "reduced vulnerability to environmental risk experiences, the overcoming of stress or adversity, or a relatively good outcome despite risk experiences."[5] However, it is a relative not absolute quality, for some children, like David, even partial recovery of wellbeing and resilience is important.[6]

Finally, in planning my work with David I was aware that building resilience is accomplished not by the removal of all risk and stress, but in the careful managing of these within a supportive relationship[7]. In addition, the path to resiliency can begin in one small part of a person's life, even from a single opportunity or turning point.

Building resiliency: David's story

David looked nervous as we waited outside the office. The door opened and I introduced him to the head teacher of a local primary school. "David is good at sports and he likes children. Could he volunteer once a week in one of your PE classes?"

Over the next couple of months, I watched a slow transformation take place. David was more focused and ready to listen to correction when things were not going so well. I think it was something about how the younger children showed their delight in having David volunteer in class that helped him change. He was doing something that he could see other people appreciated and valued. He wanted it to work. At the end of his ten weeks, David planned a dance competition for the children.

The turning point

As the day approached, I sensed David's increasing anxiety. I noticed small changes in his mood and behaviour; he became increasingly restless when meeting with me. On the day of the competition, David disappeared. Finally, I found him sitting at the back of a room in his high school, slouched all the way under the desk, in a class that he wasn't even enrolled in.

"David, listen to me. I won't let you fail. If you get up in front of the kids today and you forget what to say, I will be right there and help you."

This was the *turning point,* and success at this moment depended on my ability to reassure him and on whether he could trust me. Most children learn when they are very young that adults can be trusted to help them when they are anxious and fearful. They grow up experiencing, not perfect, but good enough, sensitive, attuned caregiving. Many vulnerable young people haven't developed this basic kind of confidence. As teachers, it is where we can provide what Louise Bomber calls *second chance learning.*[8] If we have done the work of building a relationship, a young person has the opportunity to learn something they missed earlier in their development.

The impact

The dance competition was a great success, and the pupils gave David a thank-you card. As he took the card, I watched the expression on his face. He laughed at the drawing the children had made of him and read out loud each of their names printed on the back of the card.

Later as we talked about his volunteer work, David could see how his decisions had contributed to its success. He found a sense of his own agency; he was able to bring about something positive in his life. His foster carer remarked, "He is taking more responsibility for himself. He was getting excluded and was depressed. He's happier and is in school full-time." David went on to apply to a local college to study sport's coaching.

I wish I could end the story there. A few weeks ago, I spoke to David's foster mum. She told me that after leaving school, he had gone back to his birth family, and he was now living as a drug addict.

It breaks my heart to think of David, now in his early twenties, alone and struggling with addiction. I prefer to remember him as the energetic 15-year old who wouldn't sit still and who beat me almost every time at badminton.

We must stop thinking about resilience as something we do to fix young people; it is not an event or an activity alone that makes the difference. In addition, the onus should not be on the young person to change but on the school, family, and community. Perhaps we should stop thinking about resilience in terms of the individual. We should be asking how resilience-building is our school? How do the relationships in a family that is fostering or adopting contribute to the child's resilience?

We are only ever as resilient as we are connected to those who love and nurture us and that is as true for adults as it is for children.

* Relational trauma describes the experience of chronic and prolonged traumatic events, usually of an interpersonal nature, beginning in early childhood. These experiences usually occur within the child's caregiving system and have profound developmental effects on a child.

⁴ Typically, children feel overwhelmed and powerless, and often remain confused as to the role of adults more generally.

References

1. Gilligan R. *Promoting Resilience: Supporting Children and Young People who are in Care, Adopted or in Need.* London: BAAF; 2009.
2. Luthar SS, Sawyer JA, Brown PJ. Conceptual issues in studies of resilience: past, present, and future research. Annals of New your Academy of Sciences. 2006;1094: 105-115.
3. Masten AS, Cicchetti D. Developmental cascades. *Development and Psychopathology.* 2010; 22: 491-495.
4. Van der Kolk BA. Developmental trauma disorder: towards a rational diagnosis for children with complex trauma histories. Available from: http://www.traumacenter.org/products/pdf_files/preprint_dev_trauma_disorder.pdf [Accessed December 2016].
5. Rutter M. (2006). Implications of resilience concepts for scientific understanding. *Annals of New York Academy of Sciences.* 2006; 1094: 1-12.
6. Shofield G, Beek M. Risk and resilience in long term foster care. *British Journal of Social Work.* 2005; 35: 1-19.
7. Woodier D. Building resilience in looked after young people: a moral values approach. *British Journal of Guidance and Counselling.* 2011; 39; 259-282.
8. Bomber L. *Inside I'm Hurting: Practical Strategies for Supporting Children With Attachment Difficulties in Schools.* London: Worth Publishing; 2007.

Part IV
Showing Empathy and Finding Hope

15

The Broken Toilet and the Importance of Attunement

Helping children build secure attachments in the classroom can be lot harder than it looks. Attachment theory draws from many disciplines, and it is not easy to know where to start. In addition, teachers may wonder if all of this relationship stuff is part of their job description. Attunement is probably the best place to begin, but it takes know-how, time, and effort.

One of the key bits of work that allowed the theory of attachment to take off was the research of Mary Ainsworth. From her detailed observations of mothers and infants, she showed that infants become securely attached when their caregivers are in sync with them both physically and emotionally. This gives the child the experience of being met and understood.[1]

I learned the importance of attunement almost by chance in my first teaching job in Scotland. I wasn't that anxious about meeting my new pupils, but maybe I should have been. I quickly found out that one nine-year-old boy in my class, Daniel*, was in the midst of an emotional crisis. He had been placed recently with a foster carer, having suffered years of neglect and abuse.

Daniel's difficulties in class were extremely challenging, and the only strategy I was given to help him was a point system in which he could earn or lose Golden Time (the Scottish equivalent of free time) each Friday. By Monday afternoon, Daniel had already lost all of his Golden Time. When presented with work, he would tear it up and swear at me. When challenged, he would sometimes bite deeply into his arm or tear everything off the walls of the classroom. As a new teacher, I didn't know where to start.

I remembered something from one of my lectures at university. Over the next two weeks, I wrote down descriptions of all of Daniel's challenging behaviours. I described his behaviours as if I was giving it to someone who had never met him. I focused on the detail of what each behaviour looked liked. I realise now that this disciplined approach helped me depersonalise his behaviours. When I stopped evaluating his behaviours, I was able to focus more on noticing his expression and affect.

Little by little, Daniel's behaviour in school began to change. The meltdowns still came, but they didn't last as long. I noticed when he was really upset, he didn't want me to leave. After a couple of months, the head teacher came to me, "I am changing Daniel's risk assessment so he can go out of the school and play football with the team, as long as you go with him."

What brought about the improvement? Upon reflection, I realised that the only thing that had changed was something in me. I noticed that I could tell what kind of day Daniel would have just by watching him walk into school in the morning. This awareness allowed me to fine-tune the work I was giving him. I made sure there was no mental maths on a day when he was anticipating a visit with his dad. I could tell when he was anxious or frightened.

One day he came to me and said that something was broken in the toilets. Previously I would have ignored this and got on with the lesson, but I could see that it was causing him distress. He was pacing restlessly. Was he worried that someone might get hurt or he might get in trouble? My intuition told me there was more going on here: perhaps a sense of threat that resonated with something fearful in his past. "We'll find the janitor," I said. "I'm sure he can make it safe." After that, each morning, before we began class, I would take him to look out the window, and reassure him that the plumbers that worked for the City Council were very good and would come soon. He needed adults to keep him safe; like the yellow tape the janitor put up, he needed words of reassurance backed up by something tangible. I wondered if we ever completely gave him that safety. Something about understanding his vulnerability helped me feel a profound sense empathy towards him. I was no longer afraid of his anger and violent behaviour.

What made the difference in my classroom? Daniel experienced what it was like to have an adult attuned to him. Mary Ainsworth defined this kind of sensitivity in the mothers she observed as, "the ability to perceive and to interpret accurately the signals and communications implicit in her infant's behaviour, and given this understanding, to respond to them appropriately."[2]

Simply making observations was not enough. I also had to learn to "read" the behaviours as cues in order to respond appropriately. I developed an awareness of Daniel's inner state, his thoughts and feelings, a mind-mindedness.

Attunement builds secure attachments when the supporting adult:

- Builds an extensive knowledge of a child through observation
- Is capable of perceiving things from the child's point of view
- Responds in way that shows the adult is reading the behaviour as a "cue"
- Monitors the child's response to ensure that the adult is reading the cue correctly
- Voices out loud what is going on in the child's mind[3]

This isn't something that only primary school teachers can learn to do. I remember when I was training to be a teacher, observing a teenager who looked like she was about to explode with anger. As the class approached the art room, the teacher was standing at the doorway. She was an older lady and small in stature. I remember thinking this could go badly. I held my breath.

As the rest of the class settled to work, the teacher, as if able to read some tell-tale signs, honed in on the one, angry teenager. She sat next to her and said in a quiet, chatty tone, "I was thinking about you and what you would need to finish your work. I have been saving these pens for you." It was like watching a parent of a much younger child, arranging the materials on the desk and all the while chatting away. There was an almost palpable drop in the tension. I breathed again.

Becoming attuned is foundational in supporting a child with attachment difficulties. Many other kinds of support depend on at least one adult being able to *read* the young person. Attunement allows us to act quickly to help a child who is not coping, and to offer just the right kind of reassurance. Once we can read his or her cues, we can begin the work of helping a child become more self-aware and emotionally regulated.

It is inevitable that there will be times when we get it wrong. We may miss a cue and leave the child feeling disconnected. However, having the sensitivity to repair the relationship is important; it is a vital part of the process of building secure attachments.

I am grateful for Daniel and for the privilege of sharing in a small part of his life. I fondly remember the look of surprise on his face and the sound of his laughter when I came into the classroom dressed up as a character from a story we were reading. I don't think he ever changed his mind about mental maths, but who can blame him.

*This is the same Daniel mentioned in chapter 1.

Keeping it Real: Building Attunement

1. Observe the young person and write detailed descriptions of their behaviours. Descriptions like, "He was disrespectful," don't help us notice what the young person looks like. Our goal is to train ourselves to be able to recognise subtle differences in things like facial expression and tone of voice.

2. Don't just observe behaviours that are challenging or distressed. Try to identify behaviours that show when he is settled, concentrating, happy, and relaxed. These are harder to notice because they may occur only infrequently.

3. Observe your own and others' reactions to the young person. These can also be clues to how the child is feeling. As we become attuned to the young person, we will probably pick up on their feelings of rejection, shame, and hopelessness.

4. Prioritise behaviours, but rather than the ones that cause you most difficulty as a teacher, think about which behaviours make the young person more vulnerable. When I do this, it helps me to empathise. I need to think about how his behaviours are causing him to become isolated from the kinds of relationships and experiences that children ought to be able to enjoy.

5. Use the questions in Louise Bomber's book, *Inside I'm Hurting*.[4] Here is a sample:
What makes his eyes sparkle?
Which feelings does he try and avoid?

How does he respond to help?
What happens when there is tension or conflict in the room?

Other Resources

Edward Tronick's 'Still Face Experiment' shows how sensitive children are to the loss of attunement: http://scienceblogs.com/thoughtfulanimal/2010/10/18/ed-tronick-and-the-still-face/

References

1. Van der Kolk B A. The Body Keeps the Score: Brain, Mind and Body in the Healing of Trauma. New York: Penguin; 2014.
2. Ainsworth M D S, Bell S M, Stayton D J. Infant–mother attachment and social development: socialization as a product of reciprocal responsiveness to signals. In: Richards M P M. (ed.) The introduction of the child into a social world. London: Cambridge University Press;1974. p. 99-135.
3. Meins E. Sensitive attunement to infants' internal states: operationalizing the construct of mind-mindedness, Attachment & Human Development. 2013; 15(5-6): 524-544.
4. Bomber L M. Inside I'm Hurting, Practical Strategies for Supporting Children with Attachment Difficulties in Schools. London: Worth Publishing; 2007.

16

Wondering Aloud - Building Support for Young People who are in Crisis

Swearing at the head teacher is never a good idea. How would I convince his head teacher that Ryan's problem was not his anger? In fact, anger was probably the appropriate response to all he was going through. There was something else that could help him, but it would take time and commitment. Louise Bomber in her book, *Inside I'm Hurting*, calls it Wondering Aloud. It is a powerful tool. However, it works better when we learn to use it first by noticing the emotions of children when they are more settled and well regulated.

Louise Bomber describes Wondering Aloud as the process by which a key adult uses observations of the child to think about what the child might be feeling and then comments on the meaning of those emotions.[1] This can help children with attachment difficulties become more self-aware and learn to regulate their internal states. "The only way we can change the way we feel is by becoming aware of our inner experience and learning to befriend what is going on inside ourselves."[2]

Wondering Aloud is a process:

1. Notice a change in the child's behaviour.
2. Describe this change to the child.
3. Make a tentative remark as to what this behaviour means or how it might relate to the child's internal state.

When I am using Wondering Aloud with a child who is distressed, I add a fourth step. I try to remind him or her of someone who can be a secure base for them. "I have seen your teacher help other children. I am sure she could help sort this out."

Ryan had been in and out of care all his life; he was now living in a temporary foster placement. Even as a newborn, his birth mother had never been able to offer him sensitive and predictable care. Ryan struggled with feelings of rejection, but also longed for a relationship with a mother. These conflicting emotions made it even harder for him to grieve his loss and at the same time left him longing for someone who would claim him. The unpredictability of his life left him extremely anxious and constantly vigilant. Most of his energy in class was used trying to say and do the right thing so that others would like him. The more he tried to get other children to like him, the more they seemed to reject him.

Ryan's teacher told me, "He is not coping with playtimes. He is aggressive towards the other children. He has also become much more attention seeking and I can see he is extremely anxious. Sadly, he doesn't know how to express or even recognise all the emotions he is feeling, and he deals with them through being angry with others."

We decided to try Wondering Aloud, but it didn't go quite as we planned. One morning, Ryan asked the classroom assistant, "Why are my eyes flicking?" (Ryan had been crying.)

"I can see you have tears in your eyes. I wonder if you are feeling sad. Perhaps you are missing your mum. Have I got that right?"

Ryan raised his voice, "No!"

Thinking about his sadness probably reminded him of how vulnerable he felt. He was unable to accept the empathy of the adult.

A year later, Ryan was still waiting for a permanent foster family. Tentatively, I peered through the door of his classroom. The pupils were working in groups of three. Ryan was lying on his tummy on the floor. Next to him were two other pupils. His body language was almost a mirror image of theirs. Here was a rare moment of stillness in Ryan's otherwise restless day.

Here, also, was an opportunity for Ryan's teacher to Wonder Aloud in a different way. This time she could notice a more regulated emotion and tentatively give it meaning for Ryan. "I noticed when you were working you looked just like the other two children, the way you were lying on your tummy and listening carefully. I wonder if you had a good feeling being so close to other children who were calm?"

Later, Ryan's teacher remarked, "If I notice this emotion for him, then he can begin to notice it for himself. If he can notice his emotions, it might just give him enough time to pause before allowing his anger to burst out."

Louise Bomber says, "Once a child has a sense of what their experience might mean, they are then more in a position to take control over their states, sensations and feelings."[1]

However, being able to recognise what Ryan looked like when he was not anxious, sad, or upset was challenging. With children like Ryan, those moments are quite rare. They are easily missed and yet they were vital if his teacher was to show Ryan that she was tuned in to him without making him feel more vulnerable. In addition, if Ryan could learn to accept her interest in his inner life when he was settled, then he might also accept her support more readily when really distressed.

Ryan's life didn't improve. His temporary foster placement broke down. Overnight he was moved to another foster carer. He came into school the next day and lined up his classmates. "Put your hand up if you are going to miss me!" Again, Ryan was desperately looking for someone to affirm that he belonged somewhere.

I was concerned that Ryan's behaviours would escalate. Would all the work Ryan's teacher had put in over the months pay off at this moment of crisis in his life?

Ryan's teacher met me a couple of days after his move. She commented, "He wouldn't settle to work and was in everyone's face, quite aggressive and argumentative.

I took him into the cloakroom and asked him if he knew what was bothering him. He replied calmly, 'I don't know,' and it dawned on me that he didn't know what he was feeling and couldn't put the emotions he was feeling into words."

"I said to him, 'I wonder if going through so much change has been hard for you. If it was me, I would find it very hard.' He then nodded. I asked him if he went back into class would he like me to come and sit beside him for a little while to help him settle back into his work and he replied, 'Yes.'"

Had the teacher's work to notice Ryan's inner life worked? His behaviour was still challenging and yet at a moment of crisis in his life he had been able to accept help. Learning to accept the help and reassurance of a key adult is a hugely important step for many children with attachment difficulties.

Wondering Aloud is not just a gimmick; it works because of a teacher's commitment to understand and empathise with a child. It works also because the young person learns that even his strongest emotions can be identified and understood by a caring adult.

Wondering Aloud can be used to express our curiosity and empathy. Despite all that has happened to some young people, it can still make a significant difference at the time when a child needs us most.

Keeping it Real

1. Wondering Aloud only works if you have invested the time to really become attuned to a young person. You have to be able to understand their behaviour as communication, and they have to have had time to learn to trust you.

2. Expect some resistance from a young person. Don't overuse it. When I was practicing at home, my sons would say to me sometimes, "Dad, you are doing that Wondering Aloud thing again!"

3. When you try it, observe very carefully how a young person responds. Sometimes, all I am looking for is a pause. The young person for a split second doesn't know what to say after I have Wondered Aloud, and I know it has worked just because I have helped the child be curious about himself.

4. It is very important that we don't do this to manipulate a young person. We are not trying to change them or solve their difficulties; we first want to show that we are curious and accepting of their inner lives.

References

1. Bomber L M. *Inside I'm Hurting, Practical Strategies for Supporting Children with Attachment Difficulties in Schools*. London: Worth Publishing; 2007.
2. Van der Kolk B A. *The Body Keeps the Score: Brain, Mind and Body in the Healing of Trauma*. New York: Penguin; 2014.

17 Noticing the Inner Life of a Child

What kinds of changes/behaviours can we look for?	What might those behaviours show us about a child's inner life?	What kinds of beliefs and feelings might they be expressing?	How do I help them notice this?
Slowing down, less out of seat, not rushing, pausing before responding, less impulsive	Child is able to think before he reacts. He has some awareness of himself, how his actions relate to his feelings.	"I can recognize my feelings. I am aware that others can give them meaning. I can use language to think about them."	"I noticed how much self-control you had. You took your time and thought about that." *
Listening to others more and interrupting less, less conflict with others, able to see another's point of view	Child is able to recognize thoughts and feelings in others. He can more accurately identify their intentions.	"I don't feel I need to defend myself. I can take another person's perspective."	"You worked well with the group. You listened to what others said. You were patient when it looked like the others didn't understand you."
Body language and expression is mirroring others around them	Child is able to sense the emotional tone of others and uses that to help self-regulate.	"I feel peaceful when I am with others."	"I noticed you were working just like the others, sitting so still. I wonder if you had a calm feeling being close to the other children?"
Showing emotions you may not have seen before, e.g. real joy	Child is enjoying the connection they feel with others. He is not flooded with shame or rage.	"I am learning to share my feelings with others. This allows me to enjoy making others happy."	"When you were playing that game with me, you seemed to be really happy. I felt that happiness as well."
Allowing curiosity to spark interest and learning	Child trusts a key adult. This feeling of safety allows him to explore with more confidence.	"This adult won't make me feel stupid. I can tolerate not knowing, not having to be in control."	"I noticed you seemed keen to learn about…. Thank you for letting me help you."
Smiling, looking thoughtful when praised; accepting what is said	Child is feeling pride. He is enjoying the approval of others.	"I trust you that your approval of me is genuine."	"I noticed you smiled when you showed me your work. Maybe you feel pleased with yourself."
Focused, less vigilant and less distracted	Child is feeling more secure and less anxious.	"This adult can be trusted to be competent to understand my needs. The world feels more predictable and safer."	"When I looked at you today, you were working so hard, you didn't notice I was looking at you."

*These comments are not intended as a way of praising a young person. They are designed to show curiosity and acceptance of a young persons' inner life. The way the comments are made may be almost as important as the content of what is said. Body language and voice should convey measured curiosity.

18

Helping Young People Hold on to Hope

"Oft hope is born when all is forlorn." J.R.R. Tolkien

The young teenager, the victim of another Chicago gang shooting, lay motionless in the casket at the front of the chapel. I sat at the back trying to make myself invisible, and yet I was caught up in the unfolding drama. One by one, his gang member friends paraded in front of the casket. Some looked visibly moved; others full of bravado threw up gang signs. One boy, perhaps only thirteen years old, sat transfixed when it was his time to walk with his friends to the front. Then, as if a great weight had come down on him, he buried his head in his hands. Was there ever such a picture of the vulnerability of youth? Unable to find consolation or something to help him make sense of his loss, he could only hide his face.

Young people, especially those who have suffered loss, are looking for hope, for the possibility that things can get better, for certainty about their future, and for a source of purpose and meaning. "In postmodern Europe, we are not so full of religious conviction as spiritual questions. We live our lives full of longing and inarticulate hope."[1] Our children look for the comfort and reassurance of something certain. We may have to search deep into our lives in order to help them find that kind of hope.

Richard probably spent as much time outside of the classroom as he did sitting at his desk. It was the end of the school day, and there he was again standing on the wrong side of the classroom door. Just before the final bell rang, the door opened and his teacher stepped out. She looked weary and her voice was barely audible. "Richard, it has not been a good day, but tomorrow can be better."

I remember thinking, "That took some courage." Instead of berating him for all the disruption he had caused, she offered him the possibility of change. Such a counterintuitive response takes a certain strength of character, a capacity to imagine what it is like to be a kid who is always in trouble rather than respond from her own sense of weariness.

It was Activity Week at the residential school for boys with behaviour difficulties. One group was going to France and another to a caravan by the sea. However, a small number were to be left behind. They were deemed too high risk, and so I volunteered to organise day trips for them.

The day before our first trip, I noticed one of the boys was perched up on the roof of the school building. All attempts by staff to get him to come down failed. As I walked through the front door, I casually called up, "You're coming with me tomorrow. Let me tell you what we have planned." Steven descended as deftly as a squirrel climbing down a tree.

When kids have no hope, it is not surprising that sometimes they engage in risky behaviours. From Steven's perspective, what did he have to lose?

However, it is not only the possibility of a better tomorrow that children need; those who come from families in which they have been neglected and abused may lack that most fundamental of beliefs that there is any kind of benign and cohesive meaning in their world.

I was apprehensive, to say the least, about teaching religious education to a group of teenagers, all of whom had been excluded from mainstream schools. I felt like Scheherazade in *One Thousand and One Nights*; if I could engage them by telling stories, perhaps they would spare my life. So far it had worked. However, I was unprepared for what happened.

In the weeks running up to Easter, I had been teaching about the Christian faith. I was ending the lesson with a cliffhanger: "As Jesus was hanging on the cross dying, some of his friends were watching. They had hoped Jesus would be the one to change the world. As he died, I imagine that they thought all their hopes were lost. But this wasn't the end of the story, and next week I will tell you what happened."

In an instant, two of the boys sprang to their feet. I didn't have time to defend myself. One of the boys put me in a headlock. "Tell us what happened next!" he demanded.

Their reaction shocked me; it showed they hadn't given up. They weren't acting maliciously. I had something they needed. Somewhere, beneath all the rejection and disappointment in their lives, there was still a hope that someone could tell them life has some meaning, that loss and even death are not the be-all and end-all. "A fundamental part of coming to grips with loss is connecting to some form of higher meaning, purpose, and even mystery."[2]

We should recognise young people's need for hope. They are children who suffer loss through no fault of their own, and yet they cannot find meaning, especially when they do not trust the adults who are closest to them. On a daily basis, too many children are stuck believing they cannot change the behaviours that get them into trouble, and when things go wrong they cannot be fixed. Children may come to the conclusion that fundamentally relationships are unsafe and life has no purpose.

We can't always tell young people that their future will be a happy one. However, there are some practical ways in which we can help young people learn how to hope. We can give kids a second chance (and a third one and so on). The young person who is shamed in front of his classmates on a school trip and runs away can go on the next trip but with more support. The child who swears at the teaching assistant can be shown how to repair the relationship. Like learning any new skill, it takes practice and good coaching. It requires adults to act like good parents, to remember that there are bigger, more important lessons that children need help to learn: broken things can be fixed.

Children who suffer maltreatment are especially vulnerable to losing hope in the face of separation and loss. Sandra Bloom writes in *The Grief That Dare Not Speak Its Name*: "The losses that accompany child maltreatment are cloaked in silence, lost in the shrouds of history, and largely unrecognised."[4] Such losses are often stigmatised and lack any kind of social legitimacy. In addition, "A child's exposure to deliberate malevolence at the hands of a primary caregiver powerfully confuses the ability of the child to correlate the reality of his own experience with the realities of other people.

The contradictions are shattering."[4] Survivors struggle to find meaning and hope in life, and they suffer alone.

One little boy commented after the murder of his father and the death of his mother from a drug overdose, "There is no point in being angry. I just go to my room and punch my teddy bear." His extended family were too full of shame to be able to focus on how this little boy needed to express his grief.

I recently visited a teenager who had been moved to a new foster carer. He sat on the sofa, bolt upright, his eyes cast down, and his face expressionless. I felt I was looking at someone who was trying hard not to show his pain. It was only when the new carer left the room, he asked me if he could see his previous carer. Later, when out of earshot of the child, I was told in hushed tones, "We don't think that's a good idea." He wasn't just suffering a separation; even if someone was willing to acknowledge his experience of loss and grief, this young person was probably afraid of appearing like he was hurting and needing help.

Even when children experience a loss that seems irredeemable, like the loss of a childhood, there still may be ways to reassure them. Family, community, and adults who can offer sensitive and attuned responses are vital in restoring meaning and hope. The first step is being attuned to identify subtle changes in behaviour such as increasing irritability, withdrawal, and loss of motivation. Instead of seeing these behaviours as intentionally disruptive, disrespectful, and something the child needs to fix, recognise how they link to real, unresolved issues.

I remember one young person who was moved into a children's home after his gran became too unwell to care for him. In a time of profound loss, he was thrust into a place where he was surrounded by strangers. I had known him for several years, and I could see from his behaviour at school that he had lost all motivation. One day as I was driving him home, I said something like, "I find it hard to imagine how you feel right now. It probably seems like your sadness and anger will last forever. They will never go away completely, but they won't always feel so heavy or take up so much of your thoughts."

In the moment, it may be hard to find exactly the right words, but that shouldn't stop us from helping children know that the grief they are experiencing is normal, not a sickness.[5] It is a deeply personal experience, but others can recognise it and name it. Similarly, adults play a crucial role in restoring hope by holding on to a child's future even when a young person is in a place where they can't see that future for themselves. "I know it is hard for you to deal with school right now. I just want you to know that when you are older there are still ways you can get an education."

I write this a few days after the devastating fire of Notre Dame cathedral. Great buildings, even those that demonstrate the aspirations of past generations, are limited in their capacity to inspire meaning and purpose. Having an adult who loves you and who demonstrates a belief in your future may give children a much stronger anchor for their hopes. In order to hold on to hope young people need to be reminded that their grief is part of the normal process of mourning, and that there can be life and meaning on the other side of loss.

Keeping it Real

How do most children develop a belief about the world that is safe and basically benign?

Do you see young people who have given up hope? What kinds of behaviours communicate this?

How do we avoid giving young people false hope? Does the fear of giving young people false hope deter you from reassuring some children?

When you are with a child who is struggling to see any kind of positive future, what strengths or beliefs do you draw from to help him or her?

References

1. Thought for the day, Lucy Winkett. BBC Radio 4. 16 April 2019.
2. Lewis CS. A Grief Observed. Paperback edition. London: Faber and Faber; 2013.
3. Bloom SL. The grief that dare not speak its name: part 2. The Psychotherapy Review. 2000; 2(10): 469-472.
4. Bloom SL. The grief that dare not speak its name: part 1. The Psychotherapy Review. 2000: 2(9): 408-411.
5. Bloom SL. The grief that dare not speak its name: part 3. The Psychotherapy Review. 2000; 2(11): 516-519.

Conclusion

19

Discovering What Makes Us Human

Finding grounds for hopefulness and confidence

Christians and others often dismiss psychology and therapeutic approaches in the classroom. Some say therapy is used to excuse bad behaviour and children just need firm discipline. Others may be skeptical because so much of psychology seems to have come into existence in order to understand what it means to be human without reference to their Creator God. A relational approach in the classroom is based on an understanding of how young children build secure attachments to their caregivers. While embracing the research and the theories, I also compare the science to the convictions and insight that comes from my understanding of the Bible; I believe this kind of reflection gives me a deeper understanding of both and an appreciation of some of the differences as well as things they have in common.

One of those commonalties may be our belief in the existence of the mind and how we come to know our minds. Professor Peter Fonagy traces a brief history of how modern concepts of the mind have developed in Western thinking.[1] He argues against the Cartesian view that the mind is knowable purely by means of introspection. Fonagy argues instead that our own minds are unknowable without the help of another mind. Although he is not arguing for any kind of faith-based understanding, it would seem reasonable from a Christian's point of view to infer that if I was created for a relationship with my Creator then I can only know myself fully as I relate to my Creator and as I relate to those who also are created in his image.

Fonagy's criticism of Descartes may be a little harsh. Descartes realised that in order to have certainty in the awareness of his existence he needed someone to underpin the reliability of his reasoning. He unashamedly acknowledged: "A reliable mind was God's gift to me."[2] A reliable mind with its capacity for perception of truth and rationality, although not perfect, may be one of many common graces by which God reveals his goodness to the human race. Even when we choose to live as if he is not real, God does not leave us in a world of total confusion and uncertainty. I am not trying to bring to life Descartes' proof for the existence of God; rather, that Christians would assert that understanding ourselves, having true knowledge about our minds, is impossible if we take God out of the equation.

One of the marks of this postmodern age may be our drive for self-understanding. In a purely materialistic worldview every event has a physical explanation, and we are left with what is what is called *causal closure*. Human beings are seen as closed systems, and without reference to anything non-material their behaviour is predeterminable and predictable. Some will conclude: "There are no forces outside observable laws and factors that can change us. Our sense of voluntary choice is illusory."[3] Without God in the picture, we are forced to turn ever more inwardly, as if what can save us is in ourselves. When worked through to its natural conclusion, this view of humanity leaves us with no hope of real change, only a wishful optimism. I could not teach young people if I thought that there was no hope to offer them. That hope is grounded in my belief that God exists and that he has made himself known through Christ.

As a Christian wrestling to find something that can help young people, I am willing to use what psychology has to offer, but I do so humbly, recognising that there are common graces but also that science can only ever offer an incomplete explanation of what it means to be human. Realising the value and limitations of science while at the same time having a confidence that comes from my belief in a benevolent Creator gives me the freedom to be questioning and reflective in my approach. I am forced to use God's gift, my mind.

This is my Father's world and he is up to something good

Of course, rationality is not the only basis for action. When faced with injustice, there are issues of the heart. I believe a Christian's response to the suffering of the young and disenfranchised should be fuelled with passion. Some of my deepest convictions regarding social justice were forged when I lived and worked in Chicago.

What do Chicago and Glasgow have in common? Both cities, at least the centre of Glasgow, were built on a gridiron plan. Before moving to Scotland, each week I drove a minibus up and down the streets of Humboldt Park, a neighbourhood on the near west side of Chicago. Young people would run down from their ramshackle apartment buildings and fill up the seats before being delivered to our youth centre on North Avenue. Back in the late 1980's it was still a neighbourhood scarred by the effects of arson and race riots. It was a neighbourhood under siege, a mosaic of different gangs constantly at war. There were daily shootings, mostly young teenagers shot in revenge, in tit-for-tat drive-bys.

One of my first home visits was to the apartment of a boy called Caesar. As he opened his front door, we heard the distinctive pop-pop sound of gunfire on the street below. "Let's go take a look!" I said excitedly.
Caesar with a puzzled expression on his face replied, "Wait here and I'll take you back later."

Thankfully Caesar had more sense than this naive British guy. He made me wait until everything had quieted and then led me around the back of his building and through the alley.

On another occasion, driving and listening to the news, I was dismayed when I heard that a newborn baby had been found wrapped in a plastic bag in an alley not far from where I was driving. I remember feeling overwhelmed by the enormity of the problems in the inner city. What terrible circumstances would lead a mother to abandon her newborn child? I think I even prayed as I drove, but it was one of those prayers uttered up more in defeated resignation than in hopeful faith. A few hours later, my wife told me that the little baby girl had been placed with one of our best friends. I still struggle not to be overwhelmed sometimes by feelings of futility in the face of human tragedy, but every time I see a photograph of this child, who is now a young lady, I am reminded that making a difference in one life is hugely significant.

Before we left Chicago, my wife and I decided to adopt. An African American infant girl was placed in our family. Probably because our daughter is black and my wife and I are white, I have always felt that I needed to justify our decision.

In Chicago, there was a dire shortage of foster parents and relatively few African-American families able to adopt. You probably expect me to say that it was out of compassion and love that we offered ourselves, but the stronger sentiment was probably anger and outrage. I felt indignant at the injustice and evil that engulfed the community around me. I saw firsthand the effects of poverty, drugs, and violence in the lives of many families. I felt that to do nothing was to deny my identity as a follower of Jesus Christ. To make a difference in one life out of thousands says something. It says the world should not be broken like this. It says God cares and he has done something and he will do something to redress all the wrongs. It says that human beings, especially the most vulnerable are made in his image, and they matter to God.

Anger and love don't have to be mutually exclusive. I don't mean the kind of anger that is self-asserting, that erupts when I don't get my way. The anger I felt was more like the outrage and protest that we ought to feel when life and joy are stolen from a child. It may be the flip side of a coin whose other side is love. The passion we feel in the face of injustice can be a force for healing. Love that lacks the passion to be outraged over the harm done to the one who is cherished is not any kind of love.

Just in case this sounds like the decision to adopt came from some perfect altruistic motive, I think it is important to recognise perhaps I was looking for someone who would help me feel more complete as a parent. I have wrestled with this over the years. Was I arrogant to think that I could change a life? How has my relationship with my daughter been affected by my own needs? All I can say is that over the years, I have come to love her more deeply. I have been able to see the qualities that make her unique and with that insight I find her more intriguing and lovely. If you hold back from loving someone because of the fear that the love you can offer is not perfect, please think again.

Overcoming prejudices and discovering what makes us human

The German theologian, Dietrich Bonhoeffer, expressed in words the power of this kind of love: "If we love, we can never observe the other person with detachment, for he is always and at every moment a living claim to our love and service."[4] We cannot be indifferent or passive to the suffering of others and also claim that we are followers of Jesus Christ. In order to be genuine, compassionate activism also needs an integrity that comes from a realistic assessment of our own flaws and biases. Being a Christian gives me a framework for thinking about difference and vulnerability that helps me see the humanity in others.

The bell rings and classroom doors are flung open and their occupants decanted into hallways. A diminutive figure, I will call her Sarah, makes her way towards me, jostled about in the counter flow of young people. As she passes another girl whom she has known from her primary school years, she smiles and greets her. The taller teenager glances down; she says nothing and quickly looks away. Sarah's smile is frozen but just for a moment before her face looks down. I imagine a sad voice inside saying, "This has happened before. I know what it is like to be thought of as a nobody."

I wonder why Sarah, who has suffered so much adversity in life, is treated with such contempt not only by her peers but even by some of her teachers. Is it because she begs teachers for food and money or that she writes notes in class asking people to like her? Another teacher warns me, "You know she isn't that innocent."
I reply, "Yes, she can be manipulative, but given what has happened to her in the past, perhaps being manipulative doesn't have the same meaning as if you or I were being manipulative."

I use an extreme example to make my point, but too often young people who are care experienced are treated with something stronger than dislike. There is a contempt that goes beyond a rational explanation. However, in trying to understand this reaction to perceived weakness in others, I have come to realise that as Christians we may not be as squeaky clean as we like to think of ourselves.

In 1943, while running a seminary for the anti-Hitler, Confessing Church, Bonhoeffer was arrested and imprisoned. Even in his condemnation of the Nazis and their treatment of the Jews, he was able to recognise his own tendencies toward holding contempt for others:

> Nothing of what we despise in another is itself foreign to us. How often do we expect more of the other than what we ourselves are willing to accomplish? Why is it that we have hitherto thought with so little sobriety about the temptability and frailty or human beings? We must learn to regard human beings less in terms of what they do and neglect to do and more in terms of what they suffer.[5]

It is not something foreign or alien that I despise but something that reminds me of some weakness in myself. When I think about my meetings with Sarah, I see I am tempted to be impatient, to blame her when others reject her. I remind myself that this is a young person who has suffered. What I am seeing, when she lies to me, is a disposition to use people rather than trust them. I realise that I, too, can have the same tendency, and I despise it in myself. However, unlike me, Sarah is too weakened by the rejection of others to be able to change her own misperceptions.

There is another plausible explanation for this tendency to reject those who have suffered loss. Their sadness can invoke feelings of revulsion in others. C.S. Lewis in *A Grief Observed* describes the sense of shame he encountered when he tried to talk about his loss to those who were close to him: "They look as if I was committing an indecency."[6] It is very easy to outcast young people who manifest their suffering in behaviours that are difficult to understand. As Lewis sarcastically remarks: "Perhaps the bereaved ought to be isolated in special settlements like lepers." [6]

I have to learn to look harder and savour the good things in a young person; for example, their sense of humour even when they don't mean to be funny, or their spontaneity and openness of expression. There is something good to find even when that image of the Creator is harder to recognise.

Being a Christian allows me to explore my own prejudices around vulnerability and impairment. Although being care experienced is not officially recognised as a disability, yet it carries with it many of the same connotations. Individuals are too easily defined by their history of being in care to the detriment of other character attributes. Their emotional and social difficulties are viewed as impairments that create dependency on others. Young people are treated as objects: "Things are done to them rather than them doing things."[7] Their differences are seen as a drain on resources; they are regarded as taking opportunity away from others. As one care-experienced adult expressed:

> Once a person is defined by their history in this way, they are ALWAYS defined that way. Even decades later someone who was in care will still be perceived as needy or impaired. They are not allowed to grow, to mature, in the minds of those who saw them at their lowest point.

In order to understand the pervasiveness of these stereotypes, it is helpful to think about how they manifest in popular culture. Even some of our most treasured literature is replete with stereotypes of dependency and otherness. "The tragic innocent who is used to arouse indignation and sympathy does so at the cost of reinforcing a negative image of disability."[8] But are there also hints at something more noble and human? Instead of simply looking at them as plot devices, can these characters hold up a mirror to ourselves and help us face the reality of our own weakness and dependence on others?

Charles Dickens masterfully reminds us through characters such as Smike in *Nicholas Nickelby* and Tiny Tim, *A Christmas Carol,* that the qualities of those who are perceived as weaker can draw out nobler qualities in others.[7] Despite the danger that we use the disabilities of others to reinforce our sense of normalcy, Dickens' characters never seem to be corrupted by their expressions of kindness. Seeing vulnerability in others, instead, can remind us that in the future, we will all be frail and in need of others' kindness. "There are not two 'natural' categories of dependent and independent. Everyone is impaired, and all people have areas of vulnerability. No one is more than 'temporarily able-bodied.'"[7]

Diversity and living in community with those who are different keeps us honest; it reminds us of the reality of our faults and frailty, and it helps us look beyond ourselves to find what we have in common. Without including those who are seen as weaker, we are at risk of becoming trapped in our own narrow self-interest. As a Christian I see the wisdom of inclusion in Christ's teaching regarding the church. The letter to the Ephesians teaches that God has equipped Christians in such a way that it is only when we are connected to one another that we can grow and mature.[8] When we recognise that kind of mutual interdependence, we cannot say that some, who may seem like a burden, have less value. God's wisdom is demonstrated, not by the removal of our differences, but rather through the distinctiveness of different groups and individuals, he enhances who we are together.

My Christian beliefs help me confront those prejudices around the notion of difference and see the normalcy of vulnerability and frailty. But the Bible is not content with a change in attitude only. God expresses his concern for the outcast and alien as an imperative to those people who identify as his church to reach out and embrace them. At the heart of God's appeal is something about how we identify ourselves: "When a foreigner resides among you in your land, do not mistreat them. The foreigner residing among you must be treated as your native-born. Love them as yourself, for you were foreigners in Egypt. I am the Lord your God."[9]

As Christians, we could do so much more for children who are care experienced and families whose children are on the edge of being placed in care. We know what it is like to have once been alienated but then accepted by God and brought out of isolation into a community. This should motivate us not to judge and despise the weak, but to offer them everything we have, including a place in our homes, families, and communities.

Seeing a clearer vision of the power of inclusive community

Finally, a Christian's response to suffering in others must also be driven by a vision of something better, of how a community functions when difference and vulnerability are valued and not perceived as a drain on others. Occasionally I see something in a school that inspires me because it characterises the very good. Andrew, 16, has complex support needs. He is easily distracted and finds it hard to keep up with the pace of information given in class. He often looks lost, but always polite and ready to smile. When I appear at the door of his classroom looking for him, one of his friends will catch my eye and say something like, "Mr. Woodier, Andrew is in so-and-so." It is as if his classmates collectively never let him out of their sight.

Last week, the class was preparing for a concert. One young person approached me, "Mr. Woodier, is it okay if Andrew joins us in the rehearsal?" Hardly waiting for my reply, she turned to Andrew, "Follow me!"

I surreptitiously stood in the back of the hall, and noticed that Andrew's classmates had several things for him to do. One minute he was helping with sound, the next singing in the choir. I could see that rather than being a hindrance, the other young people enjoyed having Andrew be a part of what they were doing. Perhaps I am just being sentimental, but I have a strong suspicion that Andrew helps his friends just as much as they help him. He seems to draw the people who know him into more united and purposeful activity. He puts a smile on his friends' faces. Again, I am reminded of Dickens' words: "No one is useless in the world...who lightens the burden of it for anyone else."[10]

Witnessing the suffering of young people perhaps more than anything has challenged me to think deeply about what it means to be a Christian. I have grown to appreciate how well human beings develop and heal when they are in relationship with someone who loves them and a community where they are valued. My faith leads me to be more sensitive to the bewildering nature of suffering. I see not only the loss of childhood but also the loss of a future. Every child should have a destiny, a future in which they experience the fullness of life that comes from being loved and bringing joy to others. Without faith in God, I could so easily be overwhelmed by the sadness I see in others. My conviction that God is in the world and is up to something good inspires me to reach out with confidence and hopefulness. Suffering, even of the blameless child, need not rob them of meaning.

Becoming a Christian in my early twenties opened my eyes. It profoundly affected the way I view the effects of abuse and neglect in children. It allowed me to recognise my assumptions and prejudices, and helped me look beyond difference and the discomfort of loss and sadness in others to see a shared humanity. Seeing the qualities of another human being, made in the image of God, enables me to reach out even when it is hard for that young person to accept that there is something about them that can bring joy to others.

Keeping it real

How about your worldview? Does it help you think about the assumptions you make, especially when trying to understand vulnerability in yourself and others? Does it draw you toward those who struggle to find meaning in life and yet give you confidence and hope about real change and recovery? Does it allow you to admire what is best about being human while also being realistic about the evil people can do? Does it fill you with a longing for the end of evil and suffering because of a sure hope that humanity is destined for something much better?

"He will swallow up death forever, and the Lord God will wipe tears from all faces, and the reproach of his people he will take away from all the earth, for the Lord has spoken."[11]

References

1. Allen J, Fonagy P, Bateman AW. *Mentalizing in Clinical Practice*. Arlington: American Psychiatric Publishing; 2008.
2. Cottingham J. *The Philosophical Writings of Descartes Volume III*. Cambridge: Cambridge University Press; 1991.
3. White J. *Putting The Soul Back In Psychology: When Secular Values Ignore Spiritual Realities*. Downers Grove: Intervaristy Press; 1987.
4. Bonhoeffer D. *The Cost of Discipleship*. London: SCM Press; 1986.
5. Bonhoeffer D. *After Ten Years: Dietrich Bonhoeffer and Our Times*. Minneapolis: Fortress Press; 2017.
6. Lewis C S. *A Grief Observed*. London: Faber & Faber; 1961.
7. Shakespeare T. *'Help' Imagining Welfare*. Birmingham: Venture Press; 2000.
8. Bible. Ephesians 4.
9. Bible. Leviticus 19.
10. Dickens C. *Our Mutual Friend*. London: Penguin; 1997.
11. Bible. Isaiah 25.

20

The Unfinished Work of Valorising the Inner Life

The healing potential of relationships is grounded in something that is peculiarly human and also perplexing: our hunger for meaning. It seems the meaning we try to give to our own lives is never enough. We long for an intimacy with another who authenticates us as a true person, a unique individual who brings joy to others. But even the most attuned and generous of relationships only gives us a glimpse and an expectation of something even more fulfilling and joyful.

The gift of self and the healing work of relationships is unfinished. For most of us the gift of self begins in our infancy. We find that all our behaviours can be interpreted with meaning by an adult who delights in us. For others, it may be recovered later in life through the process of discovering their inner life and entrusting that true self to the loving interest and care of another human being. Knowing something about how the self is valorised in our earliest experiences of relationship, should prompt us to enquire how the valorising of self is completed.

The child needs a relationship with an adult who is self-giving, self-abandoning in their love. But at the right time the child also needs to know that this adult has their own life that is to be affirmed and celebrated. We need to see this significant other as one who can love us freely, without us having to pretend or make ourselves into someone who exists to meet their needs. As a Christian, I believe there is one who is ultimately able to do this better than any other.

The work of valorising us as genuine selves is finished uniquely by God. If you struggle to understand what that means, perhaps consider turning the question around: How do you valorise God? You honour him when you treat him as an authentic personal being, worthy of your trust, your love, and your devotion. The challenge is that although God makes himself known to us and we can enjoy an intimate relationship with him, he is also transcendent, immeasurable, and a mystery to us. We depend on him for life, but we cannot control him. In order to be valorised by God, we have to know him, but this means taking him at his word and counting on him to keep his promises. We are required to yield to him in order to receive the gift of self.

This does not mean all our deepest longings are instantly met and the mysteries of our lives resolved. But I believe this is good news for those who have been abandoned, abused, or let down by the ones who should have loved them: "If my father and mother forsake me, the Lord will take me in" (Ps. 27:10 NRSV). The Bible has many characters who struggled with God, like Job, Jacob, and King David. God was not cold nor indifferent to their needs; rather, as they learned to trust him even when they were distressed and perplexed, he imbued their lives with meaning. In knowing God, in relationship, they found themselves.

21

Epilogue: A Challenge to Christians and an Epitaph to a World Come of Age

Limousines were triple parked outside the funeral home while a police squad car kept silent vigil from across the street. Most of those assembled were young men dressed in black suits, weighed down with gold jewellery that gleamed in the shadowy light of the chapel. I remember watching gang members walking past the coffin, throwing up gang hand signs over their dead friend. Over the years, I had known many boys who had been drawn into the street gangs, only to find that it is almost impossible to get out. What horrified me here was the realisation that even in death, the gang were claiming him exclusively as their own.

As the funeral was about to begin, the boy's father walked over to one of the gang leaders. I couldn't hear what was being said, but there were angry words being exchanged. Later, I was told that the father had asked the gang for some time for the family to be alone with the dead boy. His request being denied, the father's anguish was visible even from where I was sitting at the back.

I understand now how the death of one of their own, if not managed well, could have weakened others' perception of the gang and its monolithic control. Here was a power so strong that it used death to honour the fallen as some kind of hero to further its own cause. The other reality of the loss of a young teenage boy, a precious son, shot down in a drive-by while selling drugs for the gang leaders, could be given no place here. Was there no one to stand up on the side of the father and allow him to grieve his loss? If I had been in his place, how would I have wanted my son to be remembered?

Then out of nowhere, it seemed, a minister dressed in all the garb for the occasion, began a slow march down the central aisle. His words that should have brought comfort sounded out of place: "I am the Resurrection and the Life. Whoever believes in me shall not perish but have eternal life." Of all the people there that day, it was the minister who should have stood up for the family, but even he seemed afraid. The family, who were powerless in their grief, suffered alone.

Here was an event that epitomised what Bonhoeffer called "the world come of age": a secular world so self-assured that it has no problem using the words of Jesus, just as long as the scope and influence of those words are restrained. Bonhoeffer agonised over the demise of the Christian Church and its failure to speak out against Hitler in his rise to power. He had witnessed what happens in a world come of age that is also so self-absorbed it cannot accept the limitations imposed by any other authority than its own. A world that demands to write even its own epitaph. Bonhoeffer had seen first-hand what happened when, in order to have a voice, the church had, "conceded the right to determine Christ's place in the world"[1] and in so doing had failed to defend society's most vulnerable.

It isn't always easy to look from the outside at the world we are part of; we can be so sure of our reasons for doing things a certain way, we don't always see what is missing or question our own assumptions. How are we responding to tragedy and suffering in the lives of our young people? Are we avoiding or minimising their pain? How do we respond well to those who are suffering, if our personal faith and values are not the basis for our public lives? What is the cost of not acting with integrity?

I recently took two teenagers to visit a friend who runs a drug rehabilitation programme in Scotland. These two could have been representative of many young people who have been impacted in life-changing ways by their parents' struggles with addictions. The younger one, in a quiet voice, spoke up, "If my dad had come here he wouldn't have died of a drug overdose, and my mum wouldn't have been murdered."

There was a moment of silence, a moment of understanding, broken only by my friend, who with tears in his eyes, said: "I am so sorry, son."
Three years ago, this little lad had been part of a group at school that tried to support children who were grieving. They were told that death is like a season, and like leaves falling in autumn, it can be accepted as part of a natural cycle. This is the same boy mentioned in an earlier chapter who would go to his bedroom and in his grief and anger punch his teddy bear.

Although well meaning, the teacher and the curriculum were completely out of attunement with the intensity of anguish in this little boy's life. In order to comfort him, they tried to give him some knowledge and skills to cope, but he was crying out for more. He needed someone who could acknowledge the sadness and sense of abandonment he was feeling. Perhaps there are some experiences that simply cannot be secularised. We must engage with them more deeply and personally. As a Christian, I believe I have a basis not only for hope in the face of suffering, but also, I share in that sense of outrage. Christians do not deny the existence of unjust suffering; rather, like death, we see it is an intrusion in the created order. It shouldn't be here; it was not part of the original plan, and in our anguish, we long for justice and righteousness to be restored.

By facing the reality of suffering, especially unjust suffering in the lives of children and young people, we are able to show compassion and solidarity with them. By this solidarity in their loss and shame, we can *un-shame* them. Similarly, but to a much greater extent, God the Father's solidarity with the suffering of his Son "transforms the character of suffering: it heals the deepest pain in human suffering, which is godforsakenness."[1] According to Bonhoeffer, the aim of the Christian's life is not escape from the world. We are redeemed to participate in the world through sharing in the sufferings and powerlessness of God in this world. When he wrote: "Only the suffering God can help,"[1] Bonhoeffer wanted to challenge others to live out their faith in a world that believes it has no need of God.

There is something else about Christ's sufferings that frees us to live "unreservedly in life's duties, problems, successes and failures...throw[ing] ourselves completely into the arms of God, taking seriously, nor our own sufferings, but those of God in the world."[1] As Richard Baukham, Professor of New Testament Studies at the University of St. Andrews, so rightly points out: "The message of divine suffering would be no gospel without the message of the divine victory over suffering. The cross does not make God a helpless victim of evil, but is the secret to his power and triumph over evil."[2]

God's love is not a "need-love dominated by self-seeking desires and anxieties"[2] rather it is free, generous and self-giving. His love serves as an example for me to emulate. What kind of companionship would I be able to offer, if, on the one hand, I was lost, absorbed in the other person's sadness and despair? Either I would find myself pulling back for fear of being overwhelmed by the rawness of their pain or perversely find some pleasure in being needed. God is reached by human suffering even to the fullness of his being, but he is not the victim of evil; he willingly lays himself open to another and allows himself to be intimately affected by them even to the point where, in Jesus' dying question on the cross, "he himself takes up humanity's protest against suffering."[2]

"My God, my God why have you forsaken me?"[3]

I am retiring from teaching pretty soon, and I want these last few years to count. I want to make a difference, but I risk ending my career burnt out and cynical. I want to offer myself to others in generous companionship, but that isn't easy. It often means coming alongside others in their loss, grief, and shame. As Bonhoeffer said, it is only when we engage with God's suffering in the world that we truly learn to depend on him. It is through dependence that I find a strength to keep offering that gift of self. Opening my life up to others, doesn't inevitably lead to instability. Living in relationship with others who remind me of my limitations and at the same time remind me of my capacity to bring joy is restorative and strengthening.

A life characterised by purpose and resilience comes when personal values and faith are an integral part of my identity and how I relate to others. The greatest threat to this integrity, living authentically in the world, may be our fear of suffering, our own and others'. But on the other hand, finding that integrity can help us do what is right even when the best outcomes are beyond our control. Living authentically, not always perfectly, by acting in love and truth toward others can be reassuring and intriguing. Being curious about what makes an adult tick is probably good for kids. Not so long ago, I was walking through a busy high school chatting with the young person by my side. In the jostling mass of young people, we must have stood out. Perhaps it was the relaxed nature of our conversation or the attention the young person was giving me. I smiled when my pupil tried to explain to his classmate what my job was. Finally, with a puzzled expression, the boy asked me directly: "What kind of teacher are you?"

Much of my reading and thinking takes place in a small shed at the bottom of my garden. Sometimes I like to imagine that I have been joined in that small, intimate space by some philosopher or theologian. Above the sound of screeching magpies and dogs barking, imagine listening to a conversation between two of those theologians, Diettrich Bonhoeffer and Walter Brueggemann, as they discuss the importance of relationship and being agents of change.

Brueggemann: Being a good neighbor and by extension a good teacher, carer, and friend means relating to others at the extremities of life, attending to others in their joys and sorrows. But in order to do that well, we need have our own joys and sorrows fully valorized by others and by God.[4]

Bonhoeffer: Human relationships are the most important thing in life. If we don't experience what really makes us human, then we invariably treat others as a part of the world of things. However, the healing power of relationship is not only something for those who have suffered unjustly, and for the victims of abuse. God wants us to realise his presence not just in the face of loss and suffering, but also in life, in health, and vigour. Christ is the centre of life; he cannot be confined to those parts that we don't know how to fix ourselves.[1]

Writing from his cell and not long before he was murdered, Bonhoeffer urges Christians to relate to the world come of age on its own terms. We don't seek to belittle it or to call out what we think are its failures, but in dependence on God we live unreservedly in relationship. In this way, personal faith and integrity forms the basis for true civic and social responsibility. We can be the best and most practical citizens to our fellow human beings. Therefore, I encourage other Christians to open the hatch and reach out to young people, even if your own boat is rocked. Perhaps, more than others, we have the capacity and resources to relate to young people who have suffered unjustly without fear, but with confidence and joy.

I finish with one last story. I have been meeting weekly, during term time, with one young person for eight years. Now a teenager, he is struggling to make sense of the rejections he suffered when he was younger. Recently, after the failure of another relationship, he said to me, 'I just want someone who will be as committed to me as I am to them.'

Although on the surface, he appears hardened by the difficulties he experienced in his young life, yet every time we meet, he likes it when I give him a juice box. In that one small act, I try to remind him that I am with him, and I am listening.

This same young person knows that I have written this book. He said to me, 'Mr Woodier, if your book makes money, what are you going to give me ?'

'A life time supply of juice boxes,' I replied, and he smiled.

References

1. Bonhoeffer D. *Letters and Papers from Prison*. London: SCM Press; 2017.
2. Bauckham R. Only the suffering God can help. Divine passibility in modern theology. *Themelio*. 1984; 9.3: 6-12.
3. The Bible: Matthew 27.

Printed in Great Britain
by Amazon

76471186R00061